# CHAPTER 1 - IDENTIFYING RISK

Risk Identification Techniques
Using Brainstorming to Identify Risks

## *Risk Identification Techniques*

Risks are an inevitable part of any business venture. But risks can be mitigated or avoided so long as you first identify them. When identifying risks to your project or organization, you need to consider both the internal and external factors that may cause the risk to materialize.

The main techniques you can use to identify risks to your project are brainstorming, interviewing, documentation reviews, root cause identification, checklist analysis, and the Delphi technique. The method you choose will depend on the project you're working on, but the most effective results can be gained by using a combination of different techniques.

## Overview

As a manager, it can be a challenge to ensure your team's project is finished on time and within budget. Risks such as rising costs, new regulations, and volatile markets can all affect your project's goals. But what exactly is risk? A risk can be described as the combination of the likelihood and consequences of an event occurring. To mitigate or avoid these consequences, your organization needs to have an effective risk management strategy in place.

Risk management enables you to highlight the risks that your project is exposed to. It also allows you to develop a contingency plan to overcome them. Some of its main aims are to secure an organization's cash flow, to protect its reputation and resources, and to ensure projects stay within budget.

Risk management consists of a three-step process. First, you identify the potential risks to your project. Second, you assess the risks in terms of their probability and severity, and prioritize them accordingly. And third, you deal with the biggest risks to your project by creating an effective plan of action.

This course describes how to carry out the first step, identifying risks. You'll learn about the different risk identification techniques involved, such as root cause analysis and documentation reviews, and you'll find out when they should be used. You'll then examine one specific technique, brainstorming, in further detail. You'll learn how to prepare and conduct your session and manage group dynamics. You'll then have an opportunity to practice facilitating a brainstorming session in a simulated situation.

At the end of this course, you should be better able to identify risks to your project. And you should find it easier to overcome some of the challenges of conducting a brainstorming session.

There are four questions you must ask when assessing opportunities for your department or individual project.

The first question is, "What events would increase the

probability of the opportunity occurring?" There are many variables you may be able to change with regard to an opportunity's likelihood.

The second question is, "How can we encourage those events to occur?" This involves deciding what actions to take to improve the chances an opportunity will come about.

Once an opportunity presents itself the third question is, "How can we capitalize on an opportunity that occurs?" Make sure you have the right resources in place to get the most benefit from the opportunity.

The fourth and final question is, "How will we know when the opportunity has occurred?" Set out triggers and a timeline to measure the opportunity's progress.

As a manager, you probably have to deal with risks from time to time in your organization. Some risks are negative and may pose a threat to your plans. Others have an upside and offer positive opportunities. Whatever type of risk you encounter, it's important to deal with both threats and opportunities in an effective way.

To help deal with risk effectively, you need to put a risk management – or RM – process in place. The first stage in this process is to identify the risks you're dealing with. Stage two is to assess the risks you've identified. And at stage three you deal with the risks. This course focuses on stage three of the risk management process – dealing with risk.

When dealing with risks, it's important to choose the most efficient and cost-effective response in each case.

This course describes various ways of responding to threats effectively. So, you'll be better equipped to manage threats when they do occur.

The course also outlines various responses you could consider when you encounter an opportunity. This should help you to seize opportunities and make the most of them.

In addition, the course describes the importance of contingency planning. This involves planning responses in case risk events actually occur. It also involves assigning reserves so that the responses can be implemented when necessary.

After completing this course, you'll be in a better position to respond to the risks to your projects. In this way, you should find it easier to meet your objectives – and to be more successful as a manager.

## Internal and external risks

"Nothing ventured, nothing gained." Nowhere is this proverb more appropriate than in the corporate environment, where risk is the driving force behind almost every business venture. Although some risks may provide an opportunity for growth and development, many risks can threaten your organization's long-term financial health and sustainability. As a leader, you need to manage these risks to ensure your organization's success. And a central part of risk management is to identify and understand the risks to which it's exposed.

You may have noted that risk management is important because risks are inevitable in most business environments. Many organizations constantly face threats that come about because of technological changes, market volatility, and regulatory changes.

But what exactly is risk? Risk can be described as the combination of the likelihood and severity of an event. Risks are also events with negative consequences that can prevent your organization from achieving its goals or objectives.

Risks are driven by a range of internal and external factors. While some of these factors are within your control, others may be more difficult to manage because of outside influences.

Risks caused by internal factors are generally associated with the decision-making processes and procedures already in place in an organization. For instance, you may risk losing customers if your organization has inadequate technical support in place. Other internal factors relate to investment decisions and HR management. For example, your business may end up losing market share by deciding not to invest more in research and development.

External factors, on the other hand, are associated with forces beyond your organization's control. Typical external risk factors include volatile markets and fluctuations in exchange rates – both of which may increase the cost of importing supplies. Increased competition, new regulations, and natural events such as bad weather are other external factors that can pose a risk to your organization.

Bear in mind that some risks may involve both internal and external factors. For example, suppose your organization is planning to acquire one of its main competitors.

An internal factor related to this risk is your organization's communications procedures. Without an effective communication plan, for instance, it may be difficult to ensure your business strategy is executed properly by the acquired company.

An external factor is that the acquired company may not have disclosed certain liabilities or debts that it owes to other businesses. These debts may then be passed on to your company, increasing the risk that it will underperform.

**Question**

Match each factor to the example of risks that it corresponds to. Each factor may match to more than one example.

**Options:**

A. External factors

B. Internal factors

**Targets:**

1. Damage to property caused by flooding
2. A rival cell phone company introduces a new advanced product
3. Employees are unable to use new information systems
4. Disruptions to an organization's supply chain

Answer

Weather damage is a typical external risk factor which organizations have little control over.

Increased competition and new technology are just some external risk factors that an organization may face.

This is an internal risk factor as organizations should provide internal training to ensure employees are competent in using new systems.

This risk is affected by both internal and external factors. An internal factor is that an organization may not manage its inventory properly to meet customer demand. An external factor may be an increase in supplier transportation fees.

Dividing risks into categories is also an important part of the risk identification process. It enables you to focus on the areas that are central to your organization's success. But it also helps you to generate ideas about what the potential risks may be. The four most common risk categories are financial, strategic, operational, and hazard.

**Financial**
Typical financial risks are changes in currency exchange rates, inflation, or defaults on debt owed to a business. Other financial risks may involve budget cuts, cash flow problems, or limited credit availability.

**Strategic**
Increased competition, loss of key employees, and industry changes are just some of the strategic risks that an organization may face.

**Operational**
Operational risks relate to disruptions and system failures that may be caused by defective products or equipment. They also include supply chain problems and new legislation that requires changes to an organization's processes.

**Hazard**
Hazard risks involve accidents in the workplace or injuries caused by a company's products. Damage to machinery or premises caused by bad weather or natural disasters also falls into this category of risk.

## Risk identification techniques

By having a clear understanding of the risks facing your organization, you can take action to mitigate their impact – or avoid them altogether. But to achieve this, you first need to identify and document these risks.

There are six common risk identification techniques:

- brainstorming, which encourages group members to think creatively about risks,
- interviewing, which involves question-and-answer sessions with people who have a direct or indirect stake in the project,
- documentation reviews, which consist of an analysis of documents such as the project management plan,
- root cause analysis, which you can use to find how and why previous problems happened,
- checklist analysis, which gathers historical data from previous projects and outlines all identified risks in a single list, and
- the Delphi technique, which involves creating questionnaires to gather information from people with subject matter or project expertise.

The method you use to identify risks depends on your organization's particular project or goal. But to capture as much information as possible, it's best to use a combination of different techniques. This can increase your chances of identifying all the risks associated with your project, and give you a better idea of the scope of risks involved.

**Question**

What are the different techniques you can use to identify risks to your organization?

**Options:**

1. The risk prioritization matrix
2. The Delphi technique
3. Root cause identification

4. Brainstorming
5. Risk registers
6. Checklist analysis
7. Documentation reviews
8. Interviewing

**Answer**

The six methods of identifying risks are brainstorming, interviewing, documentation reviews, root cause identification, checklist analysis, and the Delphi technique.

## *Brainstorming*

The first technique you can use to identify risks is brainstorming. This method is appropriate when all participants are available and able to meet, preferably in one location – or if that's not possible, then through teleconferencing. It can be particularly useful as it enables participants to think creatively about risks and generate new ideas.

Brainstorming, however, has a number of drawbacks. It may be difficult to schedule the session at a time that suits all group members. Brainstorming sessions can be quite time consuming. And because personalities differ, some participants may dominate the discussion and prevent others from speaking freely. Also, when teleconferencing is used, the technology must be fast and reliable, since brainstorming relies on the free exchange of thoughts and ideas.

Consider Patrick, a sales executive at a marketing company. His team is based locally in a central office and is working on a new marketing campaign for one of the company's clients, a car manufacturer.

His team is planning to use an innovative advertising approach but wants to ensure the campaign appeals to customers' needs.

To gather as much information as possible on risks to his client's marketing campaign, he starts planning a brainstorming session. He then schedules a time when all members of his team are available to attend.

**Question**

In which of the following situations would it be appropriate to use a brainstorming session to identify risks?

**Options:**

1. Andrew wants to work with investors based in his company's regional office using text-based chat software

2. Team members at Melissa's manufacturing plant work different shifts throughout the day

3. Bhadrak's software development project involves team

members located at his company's headquarters

**Answer**

Option 1: This option is incorrect. Text-based chat software may be ineffective in promoting the free exchange of ideas between participants.

Option 2: This option is incorrect. Brainstorming might not be an appropriate method to use in this case since it may be difficult to schedule a time when all team members are available.

Option 3: This is the correct option. Since the software development team members are centrally located, brainstorming may be a suitable method to use to identify risks to their project.

## Interviews, reviews, and cause analysis

Another technique often used in the risk identification process is interviewing. This method is suitable when everyone involved has some free time and works in the same location. If interviewees work in remote offices, the interviews could also be conducted over the telephone, or by using reliable teleconferencing software. However, it may be difficult to schedule the interview if there are large time differences between the offices involved.

The interviewing technique generally involves question-and-answer sessions with subject matter experts, stakeholders, project members, customers, or end-users. The purpose of interviewing is to draw upon the experience and expertise of those who may have a different perspective of your project and highlight possible risks.

When planning your interviews, prepare a list of open-ended questions. These will help avoid yes or no answers that provide little insight into potential risks. For example, you could ask what would happen if your department's budget was cut or if you missed your project's deadline. And to ensure interviewees give as much detail as possible, you could provide them with these questions in advance, as well as with a high-level summary of the project.

The next technique used to identify risks is documentation reviews, which can be used in any project type. These reviews consist of a detailed analysis of project documents to determine any potential risks relating to project requirements.

This method is used to identify inconsistencies between proposed actions and best practices. It helps to highlight missing information that may indicate a hidden risk. If your project requires specific skills, for instance, you could check that employees have the training necessary to carry out their tasks. If employees don't have the required skills, however, this will signal a potential risk to your project.

This technique may also include an assumption analysis.

Projects are usually based on a set of assumptions, such as the right hardware being available or the project budget being calculated correctly. Project team members must first document all of the assumptions being made during the project planning process. They then identify the risks that may exist as a result of each assumption being based on inaccurate or incomplete data.

A fourth technique used is root cause analysis. This is suitable when a project similar to your current plan has been completed in the past. By taking information from a previous risk event, you can discover what happened and how it happened, and you can correlate this data to your current project. For instance, if a previous project was delayed because of defective equipment, you could examine what the defect was and find out if your current project requires the same equipment.

Consider Lucas, a manager at a computer retailer. His company is planning to incorporate a new online shopping system into its web site. Lucas is aware that there were problems implementing the previous system and believes similar problems may arise with the new online shopping cart.

To identify issues that may reoccur, Lucas reviews a checklist created during the previous system implementation. This checklist includes lessons learned from the previous project, and it provides solutions to browser compatibility issues which can help Lucas with his current project.

Lucas then reviews the implementation plan for the new system. As the new system requires additional functionality such as a best sellers product listing, he checks that this is achievable before the project deadline. He's also aware that some of the software engineers have little experience developing this kind of system. So he decides to interview some external IT consultants to find out about any security issues that may pose a threat to the new system.

**Question**

Match each technique to the situation where it may be appropriate to use.

**Options:**

A. Interviewing

B. Documentation reviews

C. Root cause analysis

**Targets:**

1. Participants in Ingrid's project group are located in their company's head office but work different shifts throughout the day

2. Richard and his team want to analyze the project management plan to assess whether their estimated budget will cover the cost of upgrading the company's IT infrastructure

3. Omar is working on a new graphic design project for a client his company has worked for in the past

**Answer**

Interviewing is a useful method in this case because participants may have time to spare but are unable to meet at the same time.

Documentation reviews are used to analyze details such as the scope and cost of projects and to discover any inconsistencies that may indicate possible risks.

When similar projects have been completed in the past, as in Omar's case, information from previous problems encountered can be used to identify potential risks.

## Checklist analysis and Delphi technique

The next technique you can use to identify risks is a checklist analysis. Checklists are generally structured using the different risk categories, such as financial or strategic. They gather historical data from previous projects and outline all identified risks in a single list. Checklists should only be used as a guideline, however, as new factors might have arisen since the last project you worked on. As a result, it's best to combine this technique with other methods to identify all relevant risks.

The final method you can use to identify risks is the Delphi technique. This typically involves creating questionnaires to gather information from subject matter experts. This makes it an appropriate method to use when participants can't meet in one place, don't have time to meet you in person, when you require a large amount of input from a wide variety of sources, or when anonymity is important.

Questionnaires used in this technique can be distributed using e-mail or your organization's web site. As this technique eliminates the need for face-to-face meetings, it removes the risk of conflict or confrontation between different participants. This enables them to give unbiased answers to questions about potential risks to your project.

Consider Angela and Werner, two managers who use different techniques to identify risks to their respective projects.

Angela's team is planning to introduce a new range of kitchen appliances into the market. To identify risks to this goal, she first creates a checklist of problems the company has encountered when carrying out similar projects in the past. Her team then isolates one problem – poor initial sales – and carries out a root cause analysis of the problem.

Werner, on the other hand, decides to draw upon the expertise of a software developers' group in which he's a regular contributor, to identify risks to his team's software development project. Since these developers are located across the globe, he decides to create a questionnaire that will help him identify any potential risks.

**Question**

Match each technique to the situation where it may be appropriate to use.

**Options:**

A. Checklist analysis

B. The Delphi technique

**Targets:**

1. Derek and his team are working on a new advertising campaign for a client their company has collaborated with in the past and have access to previous worksheets used

2. Heidi needs to consult data analysts working in different industries to complete her market research project

**Answer**

Derek and his team can use previous worksheets to create a checklist of problems that occurred in the past.

The Delphi technique is suitable in this situation as the data analysts work in other industries and don't have any direct involvement in Heidi's project.

**Question**

Consuela is a project coordinator at a recently established pharmaceutical company. Senior managers at her company are planning to introduce a new arthritis medication, and it's her responsibility to identify any risks related to this new project. As part of this process, she needs to gather information from compliance analysts located in different regional offices located in the same time zone.

**Options:**

1. Root cause identification
2. Brainstorming
3. Interviewing
4. Documentation reviews
5. Checklist analysis

6. The Delphi technique
**Answer**
Option 1: This option is incorrect. Root cause identification is generally based on analysis of previous instances of risk events. As her company has recently been established, Consuela may not have the relevant data to carry out such an analysis.

Option 2: This option is correct. Brainstorming may be an effective method to use so long as all participants are using reliable teleconferencing software.

Option 3: This option is correct. Interviews can be carried out via telephone so long as there are no significant time zone differences between the regional offices involved.

Option 4: This option is correct. A documentation review would allow Consuela to compare her company's implementation plan with, for example, existing legislation, or best practices.

Option 5: This option is incorrect. As her company has just recently started operations, it may not have developed a checklist to base an analysis of potential risks on.

Option 6: This option is correct. The Delphi technique is an appropriate method to use when project participants aren't located in the same geographic region.

## Using Brainstorming to Identify Risks

Brainstorming is an effective way of generating ideas about risks related to your team or department's project.

When preparing for your brainstorming session, define its scope and adapt the process so that your team can identify genuine risks.

To conduct your brainstorming session effectively, remind participants of the objective of the session, and establish the ground rules from the outset. Facilitate the brainstorming session by following the set rules and by using the appropriate metalanguage. Then consolidate the ideas into a list of the risks identified.

Finally, to overcome challenges such as groupthink and dominant participants, you need to be skilled in managing group dynamics and ensure that participants are committed to the session rules.

## *Preparing for a brainstorming session*

One of the most common methods of identifying risks is brainstorming. Remember that brainstorming is an effective method to use when you want to establish an open dialogue and stimulate fresh ideas.

**Question**

What do you think are the main benefits of using brainstorming to identify risks to your project?

**Options:**
1. It promotes better idea generation and solution development
2. It gives employees a feeling of involvement
3. It produces visible results
4. It's usually considered a fun activity
5. It gives employees a chance to be creative
6. It encourages team building

**Answer**

Actually, all of these are benefits of brainstorming. Select each benefit to find out more about it.

Option 1: This option is correct. Giving participants the opportunity to express themselves in a fun environment enables them to come up with innovative and original ideas.

Option 2: This option is correct. Brainstorming gives employees an opportunity to share their opinion about risks that their organization or department may face.

Option 3: This option is correct. Seeing your whiteboard or flipchart fill up with potential risks can give participants a sense of accomplishment.

Option 4: This option is correct. Brainstorming is generally conducted in a relaxed, informal environment away from the usual workplace.

Option 5: This option is correct. Brainstorming allows team members to come up with unusual and original ideas that may be considered unconventional in their workplace.

Option 6: This option is correct. Brainstorming can help team members bond with one another by creating a shared sense of ownership of the risks identified.

Despite its benefits, there are several drawbacks associated with brainstorming. Participants may be unaware of the purpose of the session. Or they may focus on issues that are unrelated to the risk. These problems, however, can be avoided by using two guidelines for preparing for your brainstorming session. First, define the scope of the session. And second, adapt the session for risk identification.

The first guideline when preparing for your brainstorming session is to define the scope of the session. One way of achieving this is by using existing documentation and historical data to provide a context for your project. Some of the main sources of information you can use are the project management plan, project scope statement, and organizational process assets.

**Project management plan**

The project management plan can provide an insight into project elements such as budget, objectives, and schedule.

**Project scope statement**

The project scope statement describes the boundaries or deliverables expected from your project. For instance, if you're planning to install new financial software, you might state that a new Accounts Payable package is one deliverable, but the related Purchasing System is not.

**Organizational process assets**

Organizational process assets include plans, procedures, historical information, schedules, and lessons learned from previous projects that can influence your current goal or project.

The next guideline is to adapt the brainstorming session for risk identification. Sometimes participants may focus on indicators of risks, rather than risks themselves. You can overcome this difficulty by using risk metalanguage, a format that helps to separate risks from their causes and effects. It takes the following form: Because of "cause," "risk" might occur, which could lead to "effects." For instance, because of the increase in currency exchange rates, import costs may increase, reducing the organization's profit margin.

Another way of adapting the session for risk identification is to use risk categories. You could, for example, use a table to list and group risks according to their particular category, such as financial, operational, strategic, and hazard.

You could also add other categories, such as security or regulatory, depending on your project type and scope. This can help to ensure that all possible sources of risk are considered.

Consider this example. Karen is the head of a software development team at a security device company. Her team is updating the company's suite of software, and she wants to identify potential risks to the development process by organizing a brainstorming session.

Karen first reviews the project management plan to define the scope of the session. She notes that the updates are required for the company's video surveillance systems, rather than its door access systems.

Karen then creates a list of risk categories to focus the direction of the brainstorming session. The main categories she outlines are financial, operational, security, and compliance.

## Conducting a brainstorming session

Once you've prepared for the brainstorming session and all participants have been invited and confirmed to attend, you should focus on conducting the session. Keep in mind three important steps.

First, remind the participants of the purpose of the session and establish the ground rules. Second, facilitate the brainstorming session. And third, consolidate the responses into a list of the risks identified.

The first step to consider is reminding participants of the purpose of the session. You could, for example, write the project to be discussed on a whiteboard at the start of the session. But you also need to establish some ground rules. The main rules are to specify the time constraints, and explain that the goal is quantity, not quality. Advise participants to avoid criticizing each other's ideas. And don't be afraid of periodic silence if it occurs.

**Explain goal is quantity**

The aim of brainstorming is to gather as many ideas as possible about risks, not to analyze them. After a significant number of ideas have been generated, you can then proceed to filter out the risks that seem unlikely or trivial.

**Avoid criticizing ideas**

Participants may become defensive if they fear their ideas will be criticized or ridiculed, thus interrupting the flow of creative ideas. Make it clear from the outset that group members should keep any judgments to themselves.

**Don't be afraid of silences**

Your brainstorming session may reach a lull at certain points, which can feel awkward for participants involved. But it's important to give them time to think about potential risks to your project.

Instead of pressuring participants, wait, and if necessary, suggest an idea of your own to trigger different ideas from your group members.

The second step is to facilitate the brainstorming session. You can achieve this by remaining within scope, following the ground rules, and using the appropriate metalanguage. To ensure participants stay within scope, you could remind them of the specific details of the project, as well as the different risk categories involved.

Throughout the session, make sure that group members are following the ground rules. If they're being critical of other people's ideas, remind them to keep their judgments to themselves until the end of the session. Or if participants are being reticent, invite them directly to share their opinion, or make a suggestion of your own to draw out more ideas.

Bear in mind that participants should also use the appropriate metalanguage when thinking of risks to your project. You could, for instance, remind group members of the format used to differentiate between risks and their causes and effects.

**Question**

Which examples demonstrate effective ways of facilitating brainstorming sessions?

**Options:**

1. Gwen points out to participants that low sales figures is a result of not properly analyzing customer needs

2. Thomas explains to one of his group members why her suggested risk is unlikely to occur

3. After a lull in the discussion, Kumar suggests that one potential risk to his group members' project is poor communication of compliance issues

4. Ingrid decides to extend her brainstorming session in order to gather more ideas on relevant risks

**Answer**

Option 1: This option is correct. Reminding group members of risk metalanguage can help them to stay within scope and to identify actual risks.

Option 2: This option is incorrect. To encourage a free-flowing discussion, it's best practice to defer analysis of risks until the brainstorming session has finished.

Option 3: This option is correct. Facilitators can overcome silences by providing their own ideas, which can spark ideas in other participants.

Option 4: This option is incorrect. Allowing your brainstorming session to run over time may cause participants to lose focus.

The final step to take when conducting your brainstorming session is to consolidate the responses into a list of the risks identified.

You could, for example, combine any suggestions that are similar, or merge risk-related ideas that are caused by the same internal or external factors.

## Carol's brainstorming session

Carol is a manager at a telecommunications company. She's identifying risks to a new cell phone service her company is planning to introduce. She has invited Julio, Yasmin, Peter, and Vanessa to a brainstorming session. She first outlines the objective of the session. Next, she advises group members that the session will take 60 minutes. She then asks them to be respectful of each other's ideas, explaining that the goal of the session is quantity, not quality.

Having outlined the ground rules, Carol continues with the rest of the brainstorming session. Follow along as she facilitates the session.

*Julio:* Well...one possible risk I guess is that we're entering a pretty saturated market.
*Julio says, tentatively.*
*Yasmin:* Look, we've already done the research on this, and we know there's still a market out there for our product. We wouldn't have made a decision like this otherwise.
*Yasmin says, snappily.*
*Carol:* Yasmin, I know this may seem an irrelevant point to you, but we need to raise as many issues as we can.
*Carol is respectful.*
*Yasmin:* I'm sorry, you're right.
*Yasmin is apologetic.*
*Carol:* And besides, Julio is on to something here. A saturated market is a factor. But I think it's a cause rather than an actual risk.
*Carol is explaining encouragingly.*
*Peter:* Yeah, the real risk is if we don't have a unique selling point.
*Peter is eager.*

In the previous example, Carol facilitates the brainstorming session effectively by reminding participants of the ground rules, such as not criticizing each other's suggestions.

She also reminds group members of risk metalanguage that can help them to identify actual risks.

Carol has finished conducting her brainstorming session. Participants have identified several risks to their company's new cell phone service. They create a list of the most prominent issues: the lack of a unique selling point; a rise in importation costs; the loss of a key supplier; product defects; a rise in supplier fees; insufficient funding; an increase in sales taxes; and lastly, poor cell phone coverage.

**Question**

Which examples demonstrate effective ways of conducting a brainstorming session to identify project risks?

**Options:**

1. Lorena points out that her team's brainstorming session will last for 60 minutes
2. Kevin reminds participants that they should consider financial, operational, and compliance risks
3. Bernadette gets group members to assess each other's ideas in terms of probability of occurrence
4. Anneka states that the purpose of her team's brainstorming session is to identify risks to their company's new merger
5. Wendy advises participants that they can have as much time as they want to identify risks to their software development project
6. Barry gets participants to combine and list ideas into different specific risks

**Answer**

Option 1: This option is correct. Facilitators should explain the time restraints to participants so they stay focused and on schedule.

Option 2: This option is correct. Reminding group members of risk categories can help them to avoid digressing, and to stay within the scope of the project involved.

Option 3: This option is incorrect. It's important that any analysis of ideas generated should be left until after the session has finished.

Option 4: This option is correct. Setting the objective of the session can help participants stay focused on relevant risks.

Option 5: This option is incorrect. Facilitators should avoid dragging out brainstorming sessions to maintain the concentration and energy levels of their participants.

Option 6: This option is correct. An important step in the brainstorming process is to consolidate the diverse ideas into a list of specific risks.

## Challenges to brainstorming

Besides getting participants to adhere to your ground rules, there are other challenges you may face as a result of different personality types and group dynamics. Dominant participants may use the session for their own agenda and prevent others from contributing. Individual creativity might be compromised due to 'groupthink.' Digression can often deflect attention from the real risks your team needs to identify.

It may also be difficult to give all participants, especially quiet group members, an opportunity to speak.

The first challenge you may face is dominant participants who might try to use the session for their own personal agenda to complain about specific issues. To deal with these participants, interrupt them politely and summarize the point they're trying to make. You could then ask them what risk this poses to your current project, and invite the opinion of other group members.

The second challenge you may have to deal with is groupthink. This occurs when participants feel pressure to conform to what seems to be the consensus view in the group.

One cause of groupthink is when team members have little exposure to outside information that could help them to identify new risks.

One way of overcoming this is by inviting outside experts. Alternatively, you could get group members to consider aspects of your project from different perspectives.

The next challenge is digression from the aim of the brainstorming session. Sometimes, participants may identify issues which are not necessarily risks, such as problems or general worries. Or they might identify risks that are outside the scope of your project. One way of dealing with this is to remind group members of the objective of the session, as well as the relevant risk categories involved. You could also use risk metalanguage so that only genuine risks are identified.

The last challenge you need to overcome is giving everyone,

especially quieter group members, an opportunity to speak. Some participants may have good ideas about possible risks but are too shy or afraid of criticism to share them.

To get input from all group members, remind them that they should defer judgment of ideas until after the brainstorming session.

If some participants are still reticent, ask them directly about their experience or opinions of issues being discussed.

**Question**
Match each action to the challenge that it helps to overcome.
**Options:**
A. Irene thanks an aggressive group member for his contribution and asks another group member to share her opinion
B. Abu gets his software development team members to imagine problems online users might encounter
C. Marianne explains that her team needs to focus on food safety compliance risks rather than its overtime payments
D. Troy asks a software programmer about her experience after noticing her reluctance to talk about previous projects she has worked on
**Targets:**
1. Dominant participants
2. Groupthink
3. Digression
4. Quiet group members
Answer

Dominant group members may try to use your brainstorming session to get their own message across. Groupthink occurs when participants reach a consensus without exploring any alternatives. Participants may digress from the aim of your brainstorming session if they start to talk about unrelated worries or problems.

Quiet participants may be too shy or afraid of being criticized to share their own opinions.

## Robert's brainstorming session

Next, you'll see how Robert, a manager at a financial services company, handles the challenges associated with brainstorming sessions. He's meeting with team members Carmen, Matsuri, and Vanessa to identify risks to a new CRM system his company is planning to install. He's also invited, Max, an external IT consultant, to help with the process. So far, they've highlighted the risk that the implementation team may have to rush because of a tight deadline, adversely affecting the quality of the new system.

Now follow along as Robert conducts the session.

*Robert:* Okay...any other ideas?
*Robert is friendly, and speaks invitingly.*
*Carmen:* Well, for one thing, support staff don't have a clue how to use our CRM system.
*Carmen is irritated and dominant.*
*Matsuri:* Yeah! I've noticed a spike in complaints, probably because support staff haven't managed client requests properly.
*Matsuri says, eagerly.*
*Carmen:* You wouldn't believe the complaints I've had to deal with lately. Delayed payments, unresolved issues...
*Carmen is irritated and dominant.*
*Robert:* Thanks... Carmen... Your point is that employees have inadequate training, which could be a risk for our new CRM system. Correct?
*Robert says, politely.*
*Carmen:* That's right.
*Carmen is smiling and friendly.*
*Robert:* Max, what do you think?
*Robert says, invitingly.*
*Max:* Well, training is important. But the bigger problem is integrating the new database. If it's not implemented properly, some data could be lost.
*Max explains, calmly and authoritatively.*

*Robert:* Okay. Any other thoughts?
*Robert says, invitingly.*
*Vanessa:* Actually... *Vanessa says, meekly.*
*Matsuri:* I'm concerned about our marketing strategy. Everybody knows customer numbers are well down on last year.
*Matsuri is worried and irritated.*
*Carmen:* I know. If it continues like this, we won't even need a new CRM system – we'll be out of business.
*Carmen says, sarcastically.*
*Robert:* Good point. We're almost out of time so let's finish it there for today.
*Robert is smiling and speaks appreciatively.*

In the previous example, Robert facilitated the brainstorming session well by dealing appropriately with Carmen, the dominant group member. He interrupted her politely and summarized the point she was trying to make. He also got input from Max, the external IT consultant. This could help participants think of other possible risks besides inadequate training, thus avoiding groupthink.

However, Robert failed to encourage quieter members of the group to speak up. He let Matsuri cut Vanessa off abruptly, which prevented her from expressing her point of view.

He also allowed the discussion to go beyond the scope of the project. The session should have focused on the risks of implementing the new CRM system rather than problems with the company's marketing strategy.

### Question

Amanda is a manager at a pharmaceutical company that's planning to produce new blood pressure medication. She's facilitating a brainstorming session to identify related risks but is concerned that her team is focusing solely on internal operational risks. One of the participants, James, has also been persistently complaining about a new QA procedure that he disagrees with.

What actions could Amanda take to manage the brainstorming session better?

**Options:**
1. Thank James for his contribution and ask how the issue may affect production of the new medication
2. Get participants to imagine different scenarios involving vendors and customers
3. Assess the operational risks group members have highlighted in terms of their potential severity
4. Tell James he should keep his personal opinions to himself until the end of the brainstorming session

**Answer**

Option 1: This option is correct. One way of dealing with dominant group members is to interrupt them politely and ask how their problem or complaint relates to the team's current project.

Option 2: This option is correct. To avoid groupthink, you can either invite an external expert or get participants to explore situations they're not familiar with.

Option 3: This option is incorrect. Remember that evaluation of risk-related ideas should be left until after the brainstorming session has ended.

Option 4: This option is incorrect. It's important to encourage all participants to give their opinion. So it's best to just interrupt the dominant group member politely and ask how the issue is relevant to the task at hand.

**Question**

Yvonne is a marketing team leader at a construction products company. She's holding a brainstorming session to identify risks to a plan to expand into the Asian market. During the session, some of her team members start to discuss rumors of possible pay cuts. She also notices that Graham, who has experience working in Asia, has remained quiet throughout the meeting.

Which actions could Yvonne take to manage the brainstorming session better?

**Options:**
1. Ask Graham directly if he has any insights into the Asian

market
2. Let participants discuss unrelated issues at the end of the session
3. Get Graham's opinion of the proposed pay cuts
4. Remind participants of the objective of the brainstorming session

**Answer**

Option 1: This option is correct. One way of getting quieter group members involved in the brainstorming session is to encourage them by inviting them to share their expertise.

Option 2: This option is incorrect. To prevent digression, you should make it clear from the outset what the aim of the brainstorming session is.

Option 3: This option is incorrect. Although asking Graham's opinion about an unrelated topic may encourage him, it's best to get him talk about his experience of the Asian market.

Option 4: This option is correct. To get group members to discuss relevant risks, you must explain the purpose of the brainstorming session.

# CHAPTER 2 - ASSESSING RISK

Risk Assessment Techniques
Assessing Opportunities
Assessing Threats Using FMEA

## Risk Assessment Techniques

Risks come in two forms: threats, or negative risks, and opportunities, or positive risks. You need to be aware of the probability of a risk occurring, and it's also important to be aware of its impact, or likely outcome.

There are many different methods for assessing opportunities. These include opportunity analysis, market surveys, research and development, and test marketing.

The two primary methods of threat assessment are failure mode and effect analysis, or FMEA, and annual loss expectancy.

There are two primary combined assessment techniques that can be used for assessing both threats and opportunities. These are strengths, weaknesses, opportunities, and threats, or SWOT, analysis and event tree analysis.

## Key concepts in risk assessment

Uncertainty is present in any business environment. Most business decisions entail risk. Each risk presents a potential threat or negative risk, or opportunity or positive risk for your organization. You can learn to assess risks that arise by becoming familiar with the key concepts involved and the primary risk assessment techniques.

You may deal with many different types of risk at work. For example, risks could be strategic, financial, or relate to day-to-day activities. They may also be knowledge or compliance based.

You can use various techniques to assess risk. Some techniques are specifically suited to assessing opportunities that arise.

Other techniques allow you to evaluate potential threats that could undermine your project's progress.

There are also techniques that can be used for both opportunity and threat assessment. Each organization and individual must choose the most suitable technique or techniques to use when assessing risk.

Whichever method of risk assessment you decide on, you must familiarize yourself with some key concepts. First off, a risk can be either a threat or an opportunity. The next risk-related concept is the probability of a risk actually occurring. And finally, the impact of each potential risk must be considered.

**Threat**

Threats are events that may negatively affect an organization by threatening its growth potential or reducing consumer or shareholder confidence.

For example, there's a possibility that a computer peripheral company will fail to finalize a new distribution deal. If that happens, the company's market share is likely to shrink.

**Opportunity**

Opportunities are events that bring about positive outcomes and benefits to an organization. Examples include an increase in new markets opening up, the development of new technologies, an increase in sales or share price, and an increase in consumer loyalty.

For instance, a sporting goods manufacturer hopes that its new promotional campaign will lead to increased revenue.

**Probability**

Each risk your organization faces has a probability. This is the assessed likelihood of the threat or opportunity occurring. A company may categorize risk in terms of high, medium, and low probability.

High probability risks would be those that have occurred before and are likely to occur again at some point. Low probability risks might be something that's very unlikely but still should be considered.

A technology firm, for example, classifies the likelihood of a competitor creating a rival product in the coming year as having a high probability. This is a risk that has occurred for the company more than once before.

**Impact**

Impacts are the results that threats or opportunities occurring are likely to have on your organization.

For example, shareholder confidence is undermined by sluggish growth, resulting in an insurance company's share price dipping. In contrast, a civil engineering firm's annual income is higher than previously forecast due to several unexpected new contracts being signed.

**Question**

Match each example to its correct risk assessment concept. Each concept may have more than one match.

**Options:**

A. An IT firm is poised to sign a lucrative contract with a new client

B. Managers at an electronics company know it's likely that another company will release a rival product next year

C. A lawsuit could result in negative publicity for a car manufacturer

D. Due to patent problems, a cell phone company has to delay the launch of its new product

E. A celebrity endorsement results in a welcome sales boost for a clothing company

**Targets:**

1. Threat
2. Opportunity
3. Probability
4. Impact

**Answer**

Negative publicity is one example of the concept of a threat, which you should consider in your risk assessment.

New clients represent opportunities that you should consider in your risk assessment.

Figuring out the probability of risks such as increased competition is a crucial aspect of assessing risk.

The impacts of threats and opportunities, such as patent issues and endorsements, should be considered in your risk assessment.

## *Opportunity assessment techniques*

You can use a number of opportunity assessment techniques to evaluate potential favorable circumstances for your organization. The most common ones are opportunity analysis, market surveys, research and development, and test marketing.

**Opportunity analysis**

Opportunity analysis involves asking a set of questions designed to increase the chances of an opportunity occurring. This process allows you to identify where in your organization opportunities exist so you can lower costs and save time or other resources.

You can then try to capitalize on these opportunities. You're probably already aware of many of the opportunities available to your organization but be aware of new ones when they manifest themselves.

**Market surveys**

Using market surveys is another means of assessing opportunities. By using consumer questionnaires, focus groups, and online surveys, your organization can gauge from the market where new opportunities lie.

A broader analysis of collected data can also reveal long-term trends that may point to opportunities for your business.

**Research and development**

Research and development is an essential aspect of many industries. It's the process of continually researching and developing new products.

Research and development is important because continuous technological development, the actions of your competitors, and changing consumer preferences may erode the market for your established products. You can turn this potential downfall into an opportunity by developing new products or production methods.

**Test marketing**

Test marketing is another way opportunities can be assessed. It's the focused testing of your company's products or services in a single city, region, or nation before they're mass distributed. The product is marketed and sold as it would be normally, but only to a specific sample market.

Demand, consumer response, the efficacy of the marketing campaign, and the distribution method can all be evaluated. Issues with the product, such as packaging or portion size, or issues with the service, such as customer satisfaction, can also be evaluated. Test marketing can help make the product have a more successful mass launch.

Consider the example of an agricultural machinery manufacturer where a senior manager, Brad, has been asked to assess opportunities as part of the company's risk assessment process. Brad first carries out an opportunity analysis. He meets the company's department heads and asks them questions. Brad is then able to build a picture of where opportunities lie, in order to make the company more cost-

effective and profitable. Lower-cost parts and more efficient logistics are two opportunities uncovered by Brad's assessment.

To further assess opportunities for the agricultural machinery manufacturer, Brad hires a corporate research firm to conduct market surveys. Established customers are interviewed about their likely future needs from the company. This helps him identify gaps in the market that the company may be able to capitalize on in the future.

Brad also wants to ensure that research and development continues to uncover new opportunities for the company. He meets with his product managers to discuss which products are in the pipeline in the department and suggests which ones might fit with projected future demand.

Brad concludes his opportunity assessment by meeting with the Marketing Department to discuss which opportunities the test marketing of a new product has revealed. The test marketing suggests that the manufacturer might secure more machinery sales by offering an extended warranty on its products.

**Question**

Match each opportunity assessment example with its technique.

**Options:**

A. A confectionery company first releases and promotes its new candy bar in a single city

B. Scientists work on discovering new products for a pharmaceutical company

C. Managers are asked to help identify where time and resources can be maximized within the company

D. Consumers are given questionnaires to help identify what new products they want from a kitchenware company

**Targets:**

1. Opportunity analysis
2. Market surveys
3. Research and development
4. Test marketing

**Answer**

Consulting with managers is one means by which an opportunity analysis can be carried out.

Questionnaires are a form of market survey that help assess opportunities for a company.

Discovering new products is one of the primary purposes of research and development within a company.

Releasing a product in a single market initially is a way of test marketing. This helps identify opportunities that may arise from the general release of a product.

## Threat assessment techniques

As with opportunity assessment, there are several threat assessment techniques. The most common threat assessment techniques in use today are failure mode and effect analysis, commonly referred to as FMEA, and annual loss expectancy. Being able to effectively assess potential threats is an important way of ensuring a business's continued success.

FMEA enables you to pre-emptively deal with product threats. This type of analysis focuses on preventing defects, increasing safety, and improving your customers' satisfaction. The analysis is usually implemented in the design and development stages. However, it can also be done on existing products.

FMEA aims to identify all the ways a product can fail. A product is a failure if it doesn't work as intended. Even simple products have many ways they can fail. Customer error in using a product should also be included in this type of analysis. You should try to ensure that your product works as intended, regardless of how the user operates it.

Each way a product can fail is known as a failure mode. Each mode has a potential effect, with some effects being more likely than others. And each effect also has a relative risk associated with it. The failure mode and effect analysis helps you identify the failures, effects, and risks within a product, and then remove or reduce them.

The other primary threat assessment technique is annual loss expectancy. This helps your company to budget for potential threats. It's the cost of replacing a damaged or lost asset multiplied by the probability of loss or damage occurring over the year.

Risks to your company's assets include wear and tear, misuse, vandalism, and theft. Each asset in your company will have different associated risks. Some risks have an impact on all your company's assets, whereas other risks affect a specific group of assets. You calculate the likelihood an asset will be lost or damaged, and then calculate how much the asset will cost to repair or replace.

The likelihood of a loss occurring can be ascertained by referring to historical data such as crime rates, weather patterns, and other things that might impact the likelihood of an asset being lost.

Remember Brad, senior manager at the agricultural machinery manufacturer? He assesses potential threats as part of the company's risk assessment strategy. Brad commissions an FMEA on a combine harvester his company is developing and calculates the company's annual loss expectancy.

The FMEA comprises numerous tests on harvester prototypes. These tests highlight a safety risk. There are some ways an operator might misuse the harvester that could be dangerous. In response to this, Brad asks the product manager to order a redesign of the operator interface and the inclusion of additional safety features in the harvester. The FMEA has uncovered a significant threat that Brad is then able to minimize.

Brad then calculates the manufacturer's annual loss expectancy. He knows the typical rate of breakdown of the manufacturing equipment and how much it costs to repair. He also factors in the risk of theft and of adverse weather damaging company assets and how much each could cost. Using these potential costs, he's able to extrapolate the company's annual loss expectancy.

**Question**

Match each example of a risk to the technique you would use to assess it. Each example may match to more than one technique and each technique may be suitable for more than one example.

**Options:**

A. A kitchen appliance company's new product may be prone to user error

B. A catering company's stock suffers from high levels of spoilage

C. If any of the hardware in a cell phone company's new product is faulty, the company may experience significant losses

D. If a tornado hit its primary manufacturing plant, a textiles company's production capacity would plummet

**Targets:**

1. FMEA

2. Annual loss expectancy

Answer

FMEA is a threat assessment technique typically applied during the development of a product, designed to minimize the risk of a product failing.

Annual loss expectancy is an opportunity assessment technique used to budget for potential threats occurring within the business.

## Combined assessment techniques

As well as opportunity-specific and threat-specific assessment techniques, you can use some combined assessment techniques to assess both opportunities and threats. One common technique is strengths, weaknesses, opportunities, and threats analysis, commonly called a SWOT analysis. Another technique is event tree analysis.

The first combined assessment technique is a SWOT analysis. It includes specifying a company's primary objectives and identifying the positive and negative factors, both internal and external, that will contribute toward those objectives. It matches the company's strengths to external opportunities and also aims to convert weaknesses and threats into strengths and opportunities. A company's strengths with one objective may be weaknesses with regard to another objective.

The second combined assessment technique is event tree analysis. An event tree is a graphical representation that shows possible results from a specific event. By creating an event tree, you can show the likely repercussions of a particular event.

Repercussions may take the form of threats or opportunities, depending on the event and the nature of your company. This type of graphic can visually highlight where a threat or opportunity may arise for your organization. It also helps you strategize about the long-term implications of events.

Getting back to Brad – the senior manager at the agricultural machinery manufacturer – he concludes his assessment by reviewing overall threats and opportunities for the company. Using the SWOT analysis, he realizes where the company can line up its best products with overseas prospects. The analysis also identifies ways to boost sales of the company's less popular product lines.

Brad continues by performing an event tree analysis to assess the outcomes of a number of likely events. Beginning with the assessment of a major new contract, he uncovers potential threats and opportunities that this contract might lead to.

He also performs an event tree analysis on equipment failure and other undesirable events. These analyses allow him to develop a strategy for minimizing the negative risks involved in any of the events.

**Question**

Match each example of a risk to its most suitable assessment technique. Each example may match to more than one technique and each technique may be suitable for more than one example.

**Options:**

A. A cosmetics company can generate more revenue by aligning its strongest brands with advertising firms in new markets

B. An insurance company charts the potential upsides and downsides of expanding into international markets

C. A car company has a lot of older stock that is likely to depreciate in value unless a new market can be identified for it

D. In case an explosion occurs at a chemical company's processing plant, its risk assessor maps out the likely outcomes

Targets:

1. SWOT analysis
2. Event tree analysis

**Answer**

SWOT analysis is a combined assessment technique that lines up a company's strengths with opportunities and aims to turn weaknesses and threats into strengths and opportunities.

Event tree analysis is a combined assessment technique whereby a graphic is created that shows the outcomes of a specific event.

## *Assessing Opportunities*

There are four questions you must ask when assessing opportunities for your department or individual project.

The first question is, "What events would increase the probability of the opportunity occurring?" There are many variables you may be able to change with regard to an opportunity's likelihood.

The second question is, "How can we encourage those events to occur?" This involves deciding what actions to take to improve the chances an opportunity will come about.

Once an opportunity presents itself the third question is, "How can we capitalize on an opportunity that occurs?" Make sure you have the right resources in place to get the most benefit from the opportunity.

The fourth and final question is, "How will we know when the opportunity has occurred?" Set out triggers and a timeline to measure the opportunity's progress.

## Opportunity assessment

In your daily work, you may encounter lots of potentially valuable opportunities. By learning to assess opportunities, you can pick those that will most benefit you and your organization. And through pursuing the best opportunities, you should be able to save money and time, and strengthen your team. All of these benefits should add value to your projects and improve your organization's long-term performance.

It's unlikely that your organization will be able to pursue every opportunity that presents itself. So how do you decide which ones will benefit you and your organization the most?

By asking the right questions about each apparent opportunity, you can assess their value. Seek the input of everyone working on your project when answering these questions and you can then decide which opportunities to pursue.

You need to ask four questions when assessing opportunities. The first question is, "What events would increase the probability of the opportunity occurring?" The second question is, "How can we encourage those events to occur?" The third is, "How can we capitalize on an opportunity that occurs?" And the final question is, "How will we know when the opportunity has occurred?"

**Question**

There are six questions in the opportunity assessment process. Is this statement true or false?

**Options:**

1. True
2. False

**Answer**

There are four questions that must be asked and answered in the opportunity assessment process. The questions relate to probability, encouraging events, capitalizing on opportunities, and identifying triggers.

## *Increase probability*

The first opportunity assessment question you must ask is, "What events would increase the probability of the opportunity occurring?" Consult your team members about the question, soliciting their opinions on how you can make an opportunity more likely to happen. This could entail loosening rigid procedures or improving communication among your team. Or it could simply mean getting the team to agree on an agenda for making the opportunity become a reality.

Consider the example of Bhadrak, a product development manager at a consumer electronics company, and his team, Lori, Frank, and Makola. They've identified an opportunity to work on new products in collaboration with a prestigious local university. The whole team wants this collaboration to come about as it could result in better visibility in the market. However, the ultimate decision lies with the university's administration. Bhadrak calls a meeting to discuss how they can increase the probability of the collaboration.

Follow along as Bhadrak, Lori, Frank, and Makola discuss improving the probability of a collaboration with the university.

*Bhadrak:* We need to make this collaboration more attractive to the university. Any ideas?

*Bhadrak is serious.*

*Lori:* Well, it's my alma mater. Maybe I could join the discussion with the university group?

*Lori is thoughtful.*

*Bhadrak:* Nice! They might listen to an alumnus! Frank... Makola... any thoughts?

*Makola:* Maybe offer the university better patent terms? It might sweeten the deal for them.

Bhadrak: True...could improve our chances of finalizing a deal.

*Bhadrak is thoughtful.*

*Frank:* And what about offering more summer internships for the university's undergraduates?

*Bhadrak:* Mmhmm...that might work too. Very good ideas, everyone!

*Bhadrak is satisfied.*

Bhadrak's meeting with his team has gone well. He has asked what can be done to improve the probability of the collaboration being agreed on. His team has offered some realistic suggestions for what could be done to make the collaboration more attractive to the university.

Bhadrak and his team have successfully addressed the first question when assessing an opportunity. Although they know the opportunity is by no means certain, they've come up with ways of improving its chances.

**Question**

The Marketing Department of a car company may be able to make a deal with a popular actor for a promotional campaign. Marketing managers have begun an opportunity assessment.

What are the first two questions the managers should ask when assessing the opportunity?

**Options:**

1. "How much will it cost to ensure the actor signs up for the campaign?"

2. "How can they make the deal more likely to go ahead?"

3. "What can be done long term to maximize the actor's benefit to the car company's brand?"

**Answer**

Option 1: This is an incorrect option. While costs will come up at some point in the process, this isn't the initial question the marketing managers should ask.

Option 2: This is the correct option. The marketing managers should ask what the circumstances are that would increase the chances of the actor signing up.

Option 3: This is an incorrect option. Capitalizing on an opportunity is important but it isn't the first issue the marketing managers must deal with.

## Encourage events

Once you've come up with events that make an opportunity more likely, the next question to ask is, "How can we encourage those events to occur?" Having previously suggested events that make an opportunity more likely, you must now work with your team on making those events actually occur. This could mean changes in working arrangements or in the scope of a project. Or it could mean building bridges with people outside your department whose expertise is crucial.

Bhadrak and the team previously came up with some ideas for making a collaboration with a local university happen. Bhadrak calls another meeting of the team in order to establish how their ideas can be turned into a concrete plan of action.

In this meeting, Bhadrak, Lori, Frank, and Makola discuss how they will encourage events to happen.

*Bhadrak:* How are we going to make these ideas happen? What about your patent idea, Makola?
*Bhadrak is inquisitive.*
*Makola:* Well, the Legal Department can draw up a letter of intent... offer the university favorable terms. Assuming senior management signs off on the idea!
*Makola is happy.*
*Lori:* Yeah, they're probably going to need some persuading to give away a chunk of our patent rights.
*Lori is a bit worried.*
*Bhadrak:* OK, I'll schedule a meeting with senior management on that right away. What about summer interns?
*Bhadrak is serious.*
*Frank:* Well, we need to decide how many students we can take in each department and then run it by HR.
*Bhadrak:* OK, you and Lori start talking to the other department heads and I'll make a call to HR.
*Bhadrak is enthusiastic.*

Bhadrak and his team have turned the ideas they had to entice the university into a clear plan of action. These actions will improve the probability that the opportunity to collaborate with the university gets the go ahead. They know what needs to be done and have set down how they'll do it.

**Question**

A soft drink company may have the opportunity to merge with a foreign rival. Senior managers are assessing the opportunity.

What are the questions the managers should ask when assessing the merger?

**Options:**

1. "What are the advantages of a successful merger?"
2. "How can the company make itself a more attractive prospect for the merger?"
3. What metrics can be set in place to check whether the merger has gone ahead successfully?
4. "What actions should the company take to make itself an attractive prospect for a merger?"

**Answer**

Option 1: This option is incorrect. At this stage managers would have already considered the advantages of a merger.

Option 2: This option is correct. This question focuses on how to increase the probability of the merger opportunity.

Option 3: This option is incorrect. While setting out metrics may be useful, it isn't something managers should be asking questions about when assessing the merger opportunity.

Option 4: This option is correct. This question focuses on encouraging events that will increase the probability of a merger going ahead.

## Capitalize on an opportunity

The third opportunity assessment question you need to ask is, "How can we capitalize on an opportunity that occurs?" To answer the question, you must assess how an opportunity's outcome can be leveraged into the maximum benefit for your project. This might mean having access to the right people, expertise, and resources. Or it could mean making sure the financial and organizational resources exist to quickly capitalize on any opportunities that arise.

Bhadrak and his team must now consider how they'll get the best return on the time and money spent on collaborating. Bhadrak arranges a meeting with the team to decide how to make the most of the partnership.

In this conversation, Bhadrak, Lori, Frank, and Makola discuss capitalizing on the collaboration.

*Bhadrak:* So, how are we going to make the most of this collaboration?
*Bhadrak is enthusiastic.*
*Makola:* I've proposed a meeting schedule so we're in regular contact with university personnel.
*Lori:* We should also set up an online discussion board.
*Lori is a little nervous.*
*Bhadrak:* Very good! Communication is very important in any collaboration like this. Anything else?
*Bhadrak is enthusiastic.*
*Frank:* I've checked with Finance and there's funding left over from last year's budget that we can use.
*Bhadrak:* That's good to hear! Good to know we'll have the money.

In this meeting, Bhadrak and his team have discussed ways they'll capitalize on the collaborative opportunity available to them.

Makola has planned regular meetings and Lori has suggested

they include an online discussion board. These means of communication will help the team maximize the benefits of its collaboration with the university.

Frank has also taken action to secure financing, which will give the team the resources to fully benefit from the collaboration.

**Question**

A power company will soon be able to use a new alternative energy technology. The company's R&D manager has been assessing this potentially lucrative opportunity and has already taken action that has secured access to the technology.

What's the next question the manager should ask in assessing the technology?

**Options:**

1. "What effect will the new technology have on the company's share price?"

2. "What can the company do to incorporate the new technology into existing systems?"

3. "What actions can the company take to make the most of the new technology?"

4. "What are the dangers inherent in the new technology?"

**Answer**

Option 1: This option is incorrect. While this issue may be a concern for the company, this isn't a question that's asked in the opportunity assessment process.

Option 2: This option is incorrect. This isn't a question that would be asked as part of the opportunity assessment process.

Option 3: This is the correct option. The R&D manager should ask how the company can capitalize on the opportunity presented to it.

Option 4: This option is incorrect. While this issue would be a concern for the company, this isn't a question that's asked in the opportunity assessment process.

## Identify triggers

The final question in the opportunity assessment process is, "How will we know when the opportunity has occurred?" You answer this question by deciding how you'll identify triggers that will indicate clearly when an opportunity has occurred. Depending on the type of opportunity, you should be able to set out likely milestones and a rough time line. You can then later use these to confirm the opportunity has occurred.

All that remains is for Bhadrak and the team to establish a time line of their expectations from the collaboration and identify the triggers they'll use to determine if their goals have been met.

Bhadrak and his team meet to discuss the triggers and the time line.

*Bhadrak:* What exactly do we want to achieve here?
*Bhadrak is thoughtful.*
*Lori:* Well, at the end of year one, we should be looking at a couple of joint patent applications. At least.
*Frank:* Yeah, I agree. Hard to predict longer-term progress but I'd like to see us with a minimum of, oh, 10 joint applications by year five.
*Frank is slightly hesitant.*
*Makola:* We should have yearly patent reviews. To keep us on track.
*Bhadrak:* OK, let's set that long-term target and circulate it to our friends at the university and set up an annual patent review.
*Bhadrak is upbeat.*

Bhadrak and his team have come to the end of the opportunity assessment process. They now know the triggers they'll be looking for in the future to confirm that the collaborative opportunity has been realized. Joint patent applications are the metric they'll use. They've also predicted the rate at which these patents will be filed.

## Assessment practice

**Question**

A television production company may have the opportunity to buy out a translation company. The television production company's localization managers have been tasked with assessing this opportunity.

What are the primary questions the localization managers should ask when assessing the buyout?

**Options:**

1. "How can the production company tell the buyout has been successful going forward?"
2. "Does the buyout represent good value for money for the production company?"
3. "What can the production company do to maximize the benefit of buying out the translation company?"
4. "What alternative opportunities exist to the buyout?"
5. "What ways could factors influencing the buyout be maximized?"
6. "What factors would increase the chances of the buyout happening?"

**Answer**

Option 1: This option is correct. This is the fourth and final question the localization managers should ask when assessing the opportunity of the buyout.

Option 2: This option is incorrect. This isn't one of the primary questions the localization managers should ask in their assessment.

Option 3: This option is correct. This is the third question the localization managers should ask when assessing the potential buyout.

Option 4: This option is incorrect. Though this question may be relevant when assessing an opportunity it's not one of the primary opportunity assessment questions.

Option 5: This option is correct. This is the second question the localization managers should ask when assessing the buyout.

Option 6: This option is correct. This is the first question the localization managers should ask in their opportunity assessment.

## Assessing Threats Using FMEA

You can use Failure Mode and Effect Analysis, or FMEA, to assess organizational threats. This technique can help you identify and prevent product and process problems before they occur.

When using FMEA to assess threats, you move through three stages. Stage one is to assign rankings for severity, occurrence, and detection to the effects of each risk you've identified.

Stage two is to calculate the risk priority number – or RPN – for each risk. The RPN can be calculated using the formula severity ranking times occurrence ranking times detection ranking.

Stage three is to prioritize the risks for action. They should be ranked in order, from the highest risk priority number to the lowest.

## Benefits of FMEA

As a manager, it's important to assess the threats you and your organization face on an ongoing basis. One technique for assessing threats is failure mode and effect analysis, or FMEA. You can use this technique to identify and prevent product and process problems before they occur. In this way, potential problems can be eliminated.

FMEA is used in a variety of areas, including production, marketing, HR, and software development. For example, you could use this technique at the product design stage to identify and prevent safety hazards. You might conduct an FMEA prior to the launch of an advertising campaign, to ensure the campaign doesn't mislead or offend customers. It's used by HR professionals to ensure organizational changes are implemented smoothly. And it's used by programmers to reduce software bugs.

There are many benefits to using FMEA. The benefits you achieve can vary, depending on your particular circumstances. Consider Lucy's situation. Her team is designing a new video game. She's just used FMEA to assess the risks that threaten the project.

By using FMEA, Lucy identifies a major risk that threatens the video game – it may be too complicated for the primary target audience to use. She also identifies changes that should be made to its design to make it more user-friendly. The game's scoring mechanism needs to be simplified. And more detailed instructions should be included.

By identifying these necessary changes at an early stage – and revising the design specification accordingly – Lucy ensures that her organization doesn't waste money developing a video game that's overly complex and doesn't sell.

And her team members don't waste time redoing their work or dealing with unexpected problems down the line. Instead, they're able to work more efficiently and are more productive.

**Question**

What benefits do you think Lucy achieves by using FMEA?

**Options:**

1. She identifies necessary change requirements at an early stage
2. She reduces development costs and waste
3. She increases her team's throughput
4. She eliminates the risk of any future threats to the project
5. She's able to charge a higher price for the video game
6. She increases customer satisfaction

**Answer**

Option 1: This option is correct. Using FMEA, Lucy is able to identify the risks that threaten her product and the changes that are necessary to address those risks.

Option 2: This option is correct. Lucy ensures her organization doesn't waste money developing a video game that's overly complex and needs to be revised at a later stage.

Option 3: This option is correct. As a result of using the FMEA technique, Lucy's team works more efficiently and doesn't waste time.

Option 4: This option is incorrect. FMEA doesn't eliminate the possibility of future risks occurring. However, it provides a way of assessing the current risks Lucy identifies.

Option 5: This option is incorrect. FMEA allows Lucy assess the risks that threaten her project. This doesn't mean she can charge higher prices.

Option 6: This option is correct. As a result of using the FMEA process, Lucy's customers are more likely to be satisfied with the product they've purchased.

## Assigning rankings

When using FMEA to assess threats, you move through three stages. Stage one is to assign rankings for severity, occurrence, and detection to the effects of each risk you've identified. Stage two is to calculate the risk priority number – or RPN – for each risk. And stage three is to prioritize the risks for action.

At stage one of FMEA, you need to assign rankings for severity, occurrence, and detection to the effects of each risk that threatens your project. Each ranking is based on a 10-point scale, with 1 being the lowest ranking and 10 the highest. It's important to ensure that your team has a common understanding of what each point on the scale represents, to ensure consistent rankings. So always establish the scales before you begin the ranking process.

First, you assign a severity ranking. A severity ranking is an estimation of how serious the effects would be to your project if a potential risk – or failure mode – does occur. Sometimes it's clear, because of past experience, how serious the problem would be. In other cases, you may need to estimate the severity based on the knowledge and expertise of your team.

Imagine you're producing an expensive corporate brochure. You know there's a risk that the brochure could contain spelling errors. Your customers might be a little irritated by these mistakes. Or, they may feel you're too sloppy and stop buying your products altogether.

Irritating your customers is moderately severe. So you could assign this effect a severity ranking of 6. However, causing your customers to stop buying your products is extremely severe. You should assign this a ranking of 10.

Remember, a risk or failure mode can have several different effects, and each effect can have a different level of severity. It's the effect, not the risk, that is rated.

You may have noted that to assign an occurrence ranking, you need to work out how likely it is that a risk effect will occur – and at what frequency. You can do this by examining projects that are similar to your current one and reviewing the risk and failure logs that have been documented for them in the past.

If actual failure data is not available, you can estimate how often the risk effects will occur. To do this, it may help to know the potential cause of each risk effect. Causes could include improper operating conditions or insufficient research. Once the potential causes have been identified for all the risk effects, an occurrence ranking can be assigned.

Again, each risk effect should be rated on a scale of 1 to 10. A low ranking should be given to risk effects which never occur, or that only occur occasionally. A higher ranking should be given to risk effects that occur frequently or are inevitable.

Consider the previous example. You could decide that the cause of both risk effects is the same: you haven't allocated enough time to proofread the brochure.

From past experience, you might feel that only a few discriminating customers will actually notice the errors and feel irritated by them. As you estimate that this effect shouldn't occur very frequently, you could assign this a ranking of 2 on the scale.

Similarly, you may also feel it's unlikely that customers will stop buying your products because of a few spelling errors. As you estimate this effect won't occur frequently either, you could assign this a ranking of 3 on the scale.

Finally, you should assign a detection ranking. This measures how likely it is that a risk and its effects will escape detection.

To start, identify the current controls that are in place to detect each risk or failure. These might include quality control, testing, and inspection cycles. If there are no controls in operation, risks are likely to escape detection. So each risk effect would receive a high ranking, such as a 9 or 10.

However, if there are strong controls in place, a risk effect is likely to be detected. So it would receive a low ranking, such as a 1 or a 2.

Turning again to the example, you could decide that you haven't assigned adequate resources to conduct a thorough quality control check of the brochure.

In this situation, you clearly have weak controls in place. As the risk effects are very likely to escape detection, you should assign each one a high ranking, such as a 9.

Ideally, all of your team should agree on the severity, occurrence, and detection rankings you assign. However, sometimes team members disagree with each other as they have their own unique perspectives and opinions. If your team can't reach agreement, you can use various methods to reach consensus. For instance, you could introduce team voting or get the process expert involved in the debate. Alternatively, you could rank risks and effects relative to each other to clarify the situation.

**Introduce team voting**

If your team can't agree on a ranking, give each person the opportunity to explain to the group what the most appropriate ranking should be – and why. After each person has contributed, team members can vote on what they think the ranking should be. Based on the results of the vote, you can then calculate the mean or average ranking of the group.

For example, if three people think a risk effect should be ranked as 6, and one person thinks it should be ranked as 10, the average ranking would be 7. After additional discussion, you may find that all your team members are happy to support the consensus ranking of 7. However, if the entire team still doesn't support the ranking, you should investigate other ways of reaching consensus.

**Get process expert involved**

If your team doesn't include a process expert, you could invite this person to join your meeting. The process expert could then review the FMEA rankings your group has suggested and provide an expert opinion as to what the appropriate ranking should be.

The process expert may provide information the team isn't aware of, which can help the group reach a consensus. However, this person should never have the final say on the rankings – your team should make all decisions in this area.

## Rank risks and effects

You could rank each risk and its effects relative to each other, rather than in terms of rankings on a scale. For example, imagine your team is analyzing five distinct risk effects. It has been unable to reach agreement on the rankings for three of these effects on the severity scale. But it has reached agreement on the other two rankings.

Put each risk effect in order from highest severity to lowest severity. Forget about the scores of the rankings for now and concentrate on the risks themselves. When they're in order, indicate the severity ranking for any risk effects the team has agreed upon. This process of ranking risks relative to each other may help the team agree on appropriate rankings for the disputed risks.

## Question

Consensus means that a majority of team members support the team decision.

Do you think this statement is true or false?

**Options:**

1. True
2. False

**Answer**

Consensus means that all team members are in agreement when it comes to making a decision. Managers should have a process in place for handling team disagreements.

## *Trying to build consensus*

As a manager, you may need to make several attempts to build consensus among your team. Consider Ling's situation. He's identified a risk to his organization – installation of a new production system may take considerably longer than expected. This means production could be delayed by a month or more. He wants to ensure all his team agrees on the severity ranking that should be assigned to this risk effect.

Follow along as Ling tries to build consensus among his team members.

*Ling:* If the new system isn't up and running in seven days, it'll have a terrible effect on our output... this should get a ranking of 10...
*Ling is concerned.*
*Rico:* I disagree... I'd give it a 4. Even if it takes a month to install the new system, it will allow us to produce twice as many units per day as before... so we'd catch up fast.
*Rico is confident.*
*Shannon:* Yes, but you have to factor in that no one knows how to use the new system. It could take months to figure it out. I'm worried... I vote for a ranking of 8.
*Shannon is worried.*
*Ling:* We're arguing for three different rankings here. I guess if we calculate the average, that would give us a score of... 7.3. But that's still way too low...
*Ling is exasperated.*
*Rico:* No, it's too high...
*Rico is determined.*
*Shannon:* It can't be...
*Shannon is confused.*
*Ling:* OK, we've all had a say...but it looks like we're not going to agree this way...
*Ling is disappointed.*

**Question**

Which method of reaching consensus did Ling use?

**Options:**

1. Introduce team voting
2. Get a process expert involved
3. Rank risks and effects

**Answer**

Option 1: This is the correct option. Ling attempts to use team voting to reach a consensus. He wants the entire team to support any decision that's reached.

Option 2: This option is incorrect. Ling actually uses team voting. Each person on the team makes a case for a particular ranking and then Ling calculates the average ranking.

Option 3: This option is incorrect. Ling doesn't rank the risks and effects relative to each other. Instead, he uses team voting to try to reach an agreement.

Ling attempts to use team voting to reach consensus among his team. However, this method hasn't worked, as his team still can't agree on a common ranking. He'll have to investigate other ways of building consensus.

## *Reaching consensus*

A few hours later, Ling meets with his team again. He's determined to reach a consensus. So this time, he's going to try a different approach.

In this conversation, Ling tries again to reach consensus with his team members.

*Ling:* You all know Annie. I've invited her to drop by today because she knows all about the new system we're installing.
*Ling is enthusiastic.*
*Annie:* Yeah...it's going to really improve things. It may take a couple of weeks longer to install... but it'll be worth it. We're getting the latest version... it should allow us to triple production almost immediately...
*Annie is positive.*
*Rico:* Triple? Wow...that's more than I thought...
*Rico is surprised.*
*Annie:* And it's so easy to use...a couple of days training at most. All in all, I'd say the risks are medium to low...
*Annie is enthusiastic.*
*Ling:* Hmm... I'm thinking a score of 5 might be about right...what do you guys think?
*Ling is hopeful.*
*Shannon:* I agree – I'm happy with 5.
*Shannon is happy.*
*Rico:* Sounds good to me!
*Rico is happy.*
*Ling:* Great – 5 it is!
*Ling is pleased.*

When Ling gets the process expert, Annie, involved in the discussion, she provides new information the team isn't aware of. And she offers advice on what the appropriate ranking should be.

However, Ling's team members have the final say on the matter. They agree on a ranking of 5. Annie's input has helped them reach a consensus.

## Selecting appropriate responses

**Question**

Your team members know there's a risk that the software program they're developing contains a bug that may cause computers to crash. However, the team can't agree on the occurrence ranking that should be assigned to it.

How should you respond in order to build consensus?

**Options:**

1. Allow every team member to state a preferred ranking and then calculate the average ranking of the group

2. Ask Harry, the process expert, to join the meeting and offer advice and guidance

3. Rank the risk relative to other project risks instead of on a scale

4. Say that Harry, the process expert, will choose the appropriate ranking

5. State that if the team can't agree, you'll make the decision yourself

**Answer**

Option 1: This option is correct. One way of building consensus is to introduce team voting. With this method, the mean ranking of the group is calculated, which may lead to further discussion and agreement.

Option 2: This option is correct. If a team doesn't include a process expert, it's a good idea to invite this person to join the meeting, to offer an expert opinion.

Option 3: This option is correct. The process of ranking risks relative to each other may help teams agree on appropriate rankings for disputed risks.

Option 4: This option is incorrect. The process expert should never have the final say on the rankings. The team should make the final decision.

Option 5: This option is incorrect. A manager shouldn't decide what rankings to assign. This should be a team activity. All team members should support any decisions made.

## Calculating RPN and prioritizing risks

Stage two of the FMEA process for assessing risks is to calculate the risk priority number – or RPN – for each risk. The risk priority number can be calculated using the formula severity ranking times occurrence ranking times detection ranking for each risk item.

First, use the formula severity times occurrence times detection to calculate a priority for each risk effect. Reconsider the example you studied previously. In this example, the risk has two effects.

To calculate the priority for the first effect, you multiply six times two times nine. This gives you a priority number of 108. If the risk had one effect only, this would be the risk priority number.

However, this risk has two effects. So you need to calculate the priority for the second effect too. Ten times three times nine equals 270.

To calculate the risk priority number for the risk as a whole, you add the priority numbers for each risk effect. In this case, 108 plus 270 equals 378. So the risk priority number for this risk is 378.

Be sure to calculate the risk priority number for all the risks associated with a particular project or process. The risks with the highest RPN should be given the highest priority when it comes to taking corrective action.

**Question**
What formula should you use to calculate the risk priority number for a threat?
**Options:**
1. RPN = Severity x Occurrence x Detection
2. RPN = Severity + Occurrence + Detection
3. RPN = (Severity x Occurrence) – Detection

**Answer**
Option 1: This is the correct option. To calculate the risk

priority number, you use the formula severity ranking times occurrence ranking times detection ranking.

Option 2: This option is incorrect. To calculate the RPN, you don't add the severity, occurrence, and detection rankings – you should multiply them.

Option 3: This option is incorrect. You should multiply all three rankings to calculate the risk priority number.

**Question**

Imagine you're the production manager in a large manufacturing company. You face a risk that one of your suppliers may fail to deliver key components on time. You've identified two effects of this risk: production may be delayed and production costs could increase. Your team has assigned a severity, occurrence, and detection rating to each effect.

What is the priority number for the first effect?

A table displays a risk that a supplier may fail to deliver components on time. This risk has two effects. It may result in production being delayed, which has a severity ranking of 5, an occurrence ranking of 8, and a detection ranking of 4; or it may result in production costs increasing, which has a severity ranking of 7, an occurrence ranking of 4, and a detection ranking of 3.

**Answer**

To calculate the priority number for the first effect, you multiply the rankings that have been assigned to it. Five times eight times four equals 160. So the priority number for the first effect is 160.

**Question**

You're still analyzing the risk that one of your suppliers may fail to deliver key components on time. You've calculated that the priority number for the second effect is 84.

What is the risk priority number for the threat as a whole?

A table displays a risk that a supplier may fail to deliver components on time. This risk has two effects. It may result in production being delayed, which has a severity ranking of 5, an occurrence ranking of 8, and a detection ranking of 4; or it may result in production costs increasing, which has a severity ranking of 7, an occurrence ranking of 4, and a detection ranking of 3. The first effect has a priority number of 160. The second effect has a priority number of 84.

**Answer**

To calculate the risk priority number for this threat, you add 160 and 84. This results in an RPN of 244.

The third stage of the FMEA process is to prioritize the risks for action. To start, they should be ranked in order, from the highest RPN to the lowest. For example, if a threat has an RPN of 745, it should be ranked higher than threats with RPNs of 400 and 167. Plotting the RPNs on a graph can be a useful way of demonstrating the differences between them.

When the risks are ranked in order, you can decide which threats to address. You could decide to set a threshold RPN. Any risk with a risk priority number higher than the threshold value should be acted upon immediately. Any risks that fall below the threshold value could be set aside for now. For instance, you might decide that any threat with a risk priority number greater than 400 is unacceptable. You would then set the threshold RPN at 400.

**Question**

You're analyzing the three risks listed in the table. You've set a threshold RPN value of 500. Which risk should you prioritize first?

A table displays that Risk A has an RPN of 161, Risk B has an RPN of 501, and Risk C has an RPN of 808.

**Options:**
1. Risk A
2. Risk B
3. Risk C

**Answer**

Option 1: This option is incorrect. Risk A has the lowest RPN and it falls below the threshold value you set. So you shouldn't prioritize this risk.

Option 2: This option is incorrect. Although the RPN of Risk B is greater than the threshold value you set and needs to be acted upon, it doesn't have the highest RPN.

Option 3: This is the correct option. You should prioritize Risk C, because it has the highest RPN. Its RPN is well above the threshold value you set.

# CHAPTER 3 - DEALING WITH RISK

Threat Responses
Opportunity Responses
Contingency Planning

## Threat Responses

It's important to respond appropriately to the risks you're presented with. When it comes to threats, there are several ways you can respond.

You could decide to take action to avoid the threat. Alternatively, you might opt to transfer the risk to a third party. Another option is to mitigate the probability of the threat occurring. You could also decide to accept the threat.

Whatever response you choose, you should always take the nature and impact of the threat into account. Also, make sure your response is cost effective and doesn't cost more to implement than the impact of the threat itself.

## *Responding to risk*

Nearly all projects are subject to a degree of uncertainty and risk. If you can successfully manage the risks associated with your projects, you're more likely to bring them to a successful conclusion. Risks are often regarded negatively – they tend to be viewed as threats that you should avoid. However, some risks offer opportunities that you should embrace. So it's important to respond appropriately to the risks you're presented with.

You can use various strategies to respond to risk in an effective way. One strategy is to try to eliminate the uncertainty that's associated with risk. Or you might decide to allocate ownership of risk to the person or group who can manage it best. You could also modify your exposure to the risk you've encountered. Finally, you might think it's best to simply accept the risk.

**Eliminate uncertainty**

Eliminating uncertainty involves removing any uncertainty that's associated with a risk. If a risk poses a threat, you should aim to avoid the risk altogether by making sure it doesn't occur.

However, if the risk is likely to have a positive effect, you should exploit the opportunity it offers by making sure it definitely takes place.

**Allocate ownership**

You can respond to risk by assigning ownership of risk to a person or group who can deal with it better. In the case of a threat, this involves transferring liability and responsibility for risk to a third party who can minimize its effects.

If you're dealing with an opportunity, it means sharing the risk with a third party who can increase the probability of a risk event occurring and maximize its effects.

**Modify exposure**

If you're in a situation where you can't eliminate the uncertainty of risk or allocate ownership of it to another party, try to adjust your exposure to it yourself. For a threat, this means mitigating risk to reduce the probability of it occurring and to reduce its negative impact.

For an opportunity, it involves enhancing the likelihood of a risk event occurring. It also involves increasing its possible impact.

**Accept risk**

In some situations, such as when risk is minor or when all possible responses are too expensive, you may decide to accept risk. Accepting a threat means taking no action to avoid, transfer, or mitigate it.

Similarly, accepting an opportunity involves taking no action to exploit, share, or enhance it. In both situations, accepting risk may require some contingency planning, where you decide what will be done in the event of risk events occurring.

**Question**

Match each response to the type of risk it's responding to. More than one response matches to each risk type.

**Options:**

A. Avoid risk

B. Transfer risk to a third party who can minimize it

C. Reduce the probability of a risk event occurring

D. Ensure a risk event takes place

E. Share risk with a third party who can maximize it

F. Increase the impact of a risk event if it occurs

**Targets:**

1. Threat
2. Opportunity

**Answer**

Threats are risks with negative effects. Avoiding risk, transferring risk to a third party who can minimize it, and reducing the probability of risk events occurring are effective responses to a threat.

Opportunities are risks with positive effects. Ensuring a risk event takes place, sharing risk with a third party who can maximize it, and increasing the impact of a risk event if it occurs are effective responses to an opportunity.

## *Avoiding threats*

To deal effectively with a threat, it's important to understand the type of threat you face and its severity. Then you can choose the most effective response. For example, you could choose to avoid, transfer, mitigate, or accept the threat.

One way of responding to a threat is to avoid it. When a threat has a high probability of occurring – and is likely to have a negative impact on your activities – your first response should be to try to avoid it.

For this technique to work, you need to be fairly sure what the outcome of the threat will be. You also need to be in a position to take whatever steps are necessary to prevent it from occurring.

For example, if you develop a new product, there may be a risk that the product won't be successful and that your organization will fail to recoup its development and production costs. To avoid this risk, you could decide not to develop any new products at all. Instead, you might concentrate on improving existing ones.

Another avoidance technique is to eliminate the cause of the threat. If the cause is eliminated, the risk shouldn't occur.

For example, imagine you need to deliver a proposal to an important new client. The proposal has to arrive before the end of the week – otherwise, it will be rejected.

There's a risk that your document could get delayed in the regular mail system and arrive late. To avoid this threat, you could deliver the proposal to the client yourself.

To avoid a threat, you can also adjust your plan so that you and your activities are no longer affected by it. So if the threat does occur, you are still able to avoid its effect.

For instance, you might decide that you want to print your company brochure on a premium type of coated paper. However, the print company tells you it has had trouble sourcing that paper type in the past. It can sometimes take weeks to arrive.

You need your brochures urgently. So you decide to adjust your plan and use a readily available uncoated paper to avoid the threat of print delays.

Question

Match each example to the avoidance technique it best represents.

**Options:**

A. Decide not to make a presentation

B. Ensure team members are paid competitive rates

C. Revise an order to ensure all items can be delivered within 24 hours

**Targets:**

1. Avoid the threat altogether
2. Eliminate the cause of the threat
3. Adjust your plan to avoid the effects of the threat

**Answer**

Deciding not to make a presentation is an example of avoiding a threat altogether. For this approach to be effective, you need to be in a position to take whatever steps are necessary to prevent the threat from occurring.

Ensuring team members are paid competitive rates is an example of eliminating the cause of a threat. For example, if the cause of people resigning – being underpaid – is eliminated, this threat shouldn't occur.

Revising an order to ensure all items can be delivered within 24 hours is an example of adjusting your plan to avoid the effects of a threat. Avoiding a threat should always be high-priority.

## *Transferring threats*

Another way of responding to a threat is to transfer it. This involves shifting some or all of the risk to a third party. This doesn't remove the threat – it simply transfers responsibility for it elsewhere.

The option of transferring risk is often chosen in order to manage financial risks. Most companies that provide this type of service, however, charge high fees. You should always consult the budget and perform a cost estimate before deciding to use this approach.

You can use various tools to transfer responsibility for the threats you face at work. For example, you can buy insurance policies, issue specially designed contracts, or request performance bonds. You could also seek guarantees and warranties from your suppliers.

### Insurance

The most common form of risk transference is insurance, where you pay a premium for protection against financial loss. It typically protects against loss due to property or vehicle damage, and business interruption – through power failures or employee injury, for example.

### Contracts

Contracts can be designed to transfer specific risks to contractors, or sellers of products or services. In these cases, a vendor accepts responsibility for the cost of failure. An example is a building contract that allows for penalties to be implemented if contracted construction work isn't completed on time.

### Performance bonds

A performance bond is a type of insurance that a contractor supplies to an organization. It specifies an amount of money to be paid to the organization if the contractor fails to deliver the promised results. This protects the organization against financial loss if work isn't completed.

### Guarantees

A guarantee is an assurance of the quality or lifespan of a product, accompanied by a promise of reimbursement or replacement if the product doesn't live up to the specified standards.

**Warranties**

A warranty is a written guarantee of the integrity of a product and of the manufacturer's responsibility for the repair or replacement of defective parts, usually for a specified period of time. Electrical appliances, for instance televisions and computers, typically come with warranties.

Consider this situation. A company that produces electrical equipment has a supplier with a reputation for providing high-quality materials – but also for delivering them late.

Getting the materials late will cost the Production Department money because of the downtime this will cause.

The production manager decides to transfer some of the risk by including stiff penalties in the supplier's contract. If materials are delivered late, the supplier will be obliged to provide a heavy discount. In turn, the money saved by the organization will help offset the losses incurred as a result of downtime.

Although using penalties in the contract is an effective way to transfer risk, it also has a downside. If the agreed delivery date is missed, it might encourage the supplier not to deliver the ordered materials at all.

In situations like these, it's essential to consider all options to establish which risk you're more willing to accept.

**Question**

Which of these responses are examples of transferring risk?

**Options:**

1. Purchase an insurance policy to protect your factory against flooding

2. Include financial penalties in a contract in case the work isn't completed to the required standard

3. Ensure your IT supplier provides you with a written warranty

4. Insist that an unreliable contractor issues a performance bond

5. Ask an administrator to organize and archive guarantees

6. Terminate an existing contract and choose a better supplier

**Answer**

Option 1: This option is correct. The most common form of risk transference is insurance, where you pay a premium for protection against financial loss.

Option 2: This option is correct. Contracts can be designed to transfer specific risks to contractors, or sellers of products or services.

Option 3: This option is correct. Many products, such as vehicles, televisions, and computers typically come with warranties.

Option 4: This option is correct. A performance bond specifies an amount of money to be paid in the event that the contractor fails to deliver the promised results.

Option 5: This option is incorrect. While it's important that guarantees are properly stored, transferring risk involves making sure you receive a guarantee in the first place.

Option 6: This option is incorrect. This is an example of avoiding a threat, not transferring it.

## Mitigating threats

A third way of responding to threats is to mitigate the effects of them. This involves reducing the probability that they'll occur – and reducing the impact they'll have if they do occur – to acceptable levels. You should aim to mitigate threats when avoiding or transferring them isn't feasible, or when these responses are too costly. Mitigation tends to be the most common risk response that managers use.

There are various techniques you can use to mitigate threats:

- you can adopt less-complex processes,
- you can conduct more tests on a product or service,
- you can choose more-stable suppliers, and
- you can build redundancy into a system so that if one part fails, another part takes over its function.

**Adopt less-complex processes**

A manager in charge of distributing charity funds realizes that errors in the printing, distribution, and processing of application forms could result in the delayed or incorrect distribution of the funds. To mitigate this risk, the manager's team develops an application form that can be accessed, completed, and submitted online.

**Conduct more tests**

Before a new computer game is released, senior managers in a gaming company invite a target group to test a trial version of the game. Comments from the members of the group are fed back to the design team, which improves the game. This mitigates the risk that the game will fail to satisfy consumers who buy it once it's released.

**Choose a more-stable supplier**

If a project is at risk of late or unreliable deliveries from suppliers, choosing a reputable supplier with a proven track record can mitigate the risk. Problems with deliveries may still occur, but they're less likely.

**Build redundancy into a system**

# RISK MANAGEMENT

Computer and network systems often include redundant features to mitigate the risk of system failures. For instance, one server may automatically take over the functions of another server that fails.

As another example, the designers of a ski lift may set up a backup power supply to ensure that the lift can continue operating if the main power supply fails. This mitigates the risk of passengers being trapped in the event of a power outage.

Managers often use mitigation to respond to a threat – and taking early action to reduce risks is much more effective than trying to repair the damage after negative effects occur. However, mitigating threats doesn't eliminate them altogether.

**Question**
Which statements are examples of mitigating a threat?
**Options:**
1. Reduce the chain of command in your division
2. Invite a consumer panel to use a new product before it's launched
3. Choose a supplier who has won an award for outstanding service
4. Ensure your manufacturing plant has a backup generator
5. Turn down a request by a journalist for an interview
6. Insist that a new piece of machinery comes with a guarantee

**Answer**
Option 1: This option is correct. Reducing the chain of command in your division is an example of adopting less-complex procedures. This can help to mitigate the threat of confusion.

Option 2: This option is correct. Inviting a consumer panel to use a new product before it's launched is an example of conducting more tests. This mitigates the threat that a product will fail to satisfy consumers when it's launched.

Option 3: This option is correct. Choosing a supplier who has won an award for outstanding service is an example of choosing a more-stable supplier. By using a reputable supplier with a proven track record, you mitigate the threat of delivery problems.

Option 4: This option is correct. Ensuring your manufacturing plant has a backup generator is an example of building redundancy into a system. This mitigates the risk of system failures in the event of a power outage.

Option 5: This option is incorrect. This is an example of avoiding a threat, not mitigating it. You should mitigate threats when avoiding or transferring them isn't feasible.

Option 6: This option is incorrect. This is an example of transferring a threat, not mitigating it. Mitigation involves reducing the probability of threats occurring – and reducing the impact they'll have if they do occur – to acceptable levels.

## Accepting threats

Another way of responding to a threat is to simply accept it. Acceptance is an appropriate response when a threat is small, unavoidable, or unknown – or when it can't be avoided, transferred, or mitigated. In such situations, you might simply hope for the best and plan to respond appropriately to any consequences that arise. There are two kinds of acceptance – passive and active.

### Passive

Passive acceptance involves doing nothing unless a threat occurs, and then dealing with the consequences. For example, it sometimes rains during construction projects. The planning team may try to schedule major outdoor tasks for nonrainy seasons, but ultimately the risk of an occasional rainy day must be accepted.

### Active

Active acceptance involves accepting a threat but planning beforehand how to deal with the consequences if the threat occurs. Simply put, the management team accepts a threat until it occurs and then implements a backup plan.

Say you're due to go on a business trip and a colleague warns you that there may be roadwork on a particular highway. You could choose to include the affected highway in your route and just accept any delays. This is passive acceptance. You could also choose to map an alternate route for use only if you actually reach roadwork and find the delays are likely to be long. This is an example of active risk acceptance.

As well as planning, active risk acceptance involves making sure enough reserves are set aside to put the plans in motion if they're needed. These are known as contingency reserves. They can include money and time.

Consider this example. A manufacturing company faces the risk of a strike by its production workers. The risk management team chooses to accept this risk but also to create a contingency plan. The plan involves bringing in new, temporary labor if a strike occurs so that production can continue.

The plan also includes putting aside enough time and money to hire the temporary workers as part of the project's contingency reserves.

**Question**

Match each example to the threat response it represents. Each threat response can have more than one match.

**Options:**
A. Avoid
B. Transfer
C. Mitigate
D. Accept

**Targets:**
1. Remove an element likely to prove too costly from a business plan
2. Only purchase equipment that comes with three-year warranties or longer
3. Conduct two extra rounds of quality testing on a new product
4. Ignore the risk that an employee may resign midway through a project
5. Make a copy of an important document in case the original gets lost
6. Hope the new laptop you purchased won't be defective

**Answer**

Removing an element that's likely to prove too costly from a business plan is an example of adjusting a plan to avoid the effect of a threat. High-probability, high-impact threats are best avoided.

Only purchasing equipment that comes with three-year warranties or longer is an example of transferring risk. This involves shifting some or all of the risk to a third party.

Conducting two extra rounds of quality testing on a new product is an example of mitigating risk. Improving an ordering system to reduce the need for data to be entered multiple times is another example. Mitigation involves reducing the probability that threats will occur – and the impact they'll have if they do – to acceptable levels.

Ignoring the risk that an employee may resign midway through a project is an example of passively accepting a risk. If a risk is small or unavoidable, it may be best to simply accept it.

Making a copy in case the original gets lost is n example of active risk acceptance. Making a copy doesn't eliminate or reduce the probability that the document will get lost. However, it provides you with a backup plan to deal with the risk if it occurs.

Hoping a new purchase won't be defective is an example of passive risk acceptance. There's only a small chance that a new laptop will be defective. So it's probably not worth the effort to anticipate the problem and do something about it.

## Characteristics of effective responses

As a manager, it's important to respond to threats effectively and quickly. To do this, you need to understand the type of risks being taken in your organization. You also need to recognize the level of risk that's embedded in your processes and procedures. Then you can choose the most effective response.

To respond effectively, you should take your organization's risk management policy into account. This document sets out the organization's approach to risk management. So if it includes a section on risk responses, be sure to familiarize yourself with it and follow any stated guidelines.

You should also consider the nature and impact of the threat. For instance, a serious risk might require a crisis response – where a project can't proceed without the risk being addressed – whereas a minor risk might not require any response at all.

It's also important to ensure that a threat response is cost effective and makes financial sense. For example, if the cost of mitigating a risk costs more than the risk itself, it doesn't make sense to respond in this way.

Every threat response should have an agreed budget. So a cost-effective response is one where the amount of time, effort, and money spent on addressing the risk doesn't exceed the available budget. It also shouldn't cost more than the impact of the risk itself. So, for example, if there's a risk you might miss a flight due to traffic jams, allowing an extra 20 minutes for your journey is a cost-effective response.

Consider this situation. You need to bring $10,000 worth of equipment to a three-day trade fair. There's a risk that some of the equipment might get lost or stolen at the fair.

You could respond by avoiding the trade fair altogether. However, this could potentially cost you $50,000 in new contracts. You could transfer the risk by spending $400 to purchase insurance for the full value of all the equipment.

Another option is to mitigate the risk by bringing several

employees with you to the fair, to safeguard the equipment. Costs for this option could amount to $1,200. Finally, you could set aside a contingency reserve of $12,000 to purchase new equipment in the event it gets stolen – and to cover the time and effort of replacing it.

When you examine these responses, the most cost-effective option is clearly to transfer the risk by insuring the equipment. So transference is the best response in this situation.

**Question**
What are the characteristics of an effective risk response?
**Options:**
1. You follow the guidelines set out in your organization's risk management policy
2. You consider the nature of the threat and the impact it's likely to have
3. Your response is cost effective and makes financial sense
4. You avoid dealing with the threat for as long as possible
5. You avoid telling colleagues about the threat you're trying to address

**Answer**
Option 1: This option is correct. You should take your organization's risk management policy into account. This document sets out the organization's approach to risk management.

Option 2: This option is correct. A serious threat might require an urgent response. However, a minor risk might not require any response at all.

Option 3: This option is correct. A cost-effective response is one where the amount of time, effort, and money spent on addressing the risk doesn't exceed the available budget – or cost more than the impact of the risk itself.

Option 4: This option is incorrect. It's usually better to take action as early as possible. This reduces the probability and impact of the threat.

Option 5: This option is incorrect. Responding to a threat isn't a secret activity. You should inform any colleagues who may be threatened by it.

## *Opportunity Responses*

When you face an opportunity, there are various responses you should consider. You could decide to exploit the opportunity to ensure it occurs. Another option is to share the opportunity with another party. Or you might choose to enhance the opportunity you're dealing with. Alternatively, you could decide the best course of action is simply to accept the opportunity and move on.

When dealing with an opportunity, always examine the various responses you could make before deciding on the best course of action.

## *Exploiting and sharing opportunities*

Sometimes, when uncertainty strikes, you may receive a welcome surprise. While some risks undoubtedly have negative consequences, others have unexpected positive effects. Launching a new product could be regarded as a positive risk, or opportunity, to double your investment. A merger could be viewed as an opportunity to revitalize your organization. Try to seize opportunities when they arise – this should help you achieve your objectives more easily.

When you encounter an opportunity, you should consider how best to respond to it. You could decide to exploit the opportunity to ensure it occurs. Another option is to share the opportunity with a third party. You might choose to enhance the opportunity you're dealing with. Alternatively, you could decide the best course of action is simply to accept the opportunity and move forward.

Exploiting an opportunity involves making the most of it by eliminating uncertainty to ensure that it definitely happens.

Exploiting an opportunity could involve changing a project's objectives, schedule, or budget. You might achieve this by reducing the time period to complete a project by bringing in more qualified resources or by improving the level of quality that was originally planned.

The exploit response might even involve managing a project in a completely different way than was originally planned. Whatever approach you take, you don't leave the opportunity to chance. You make a positive decision to include the potential opportunity in the scope of your project and you ensure it's not missed.

**Question**

When you face an opportunity, the first response you consider should be to exploit it.

Do you think this statement is true or false?
**Options:**
1. True

2. False

**Answer**

It's generally accepted that you should try to exploit opportunities before you attempt to share, enhance, or accept them.

Consider this example. A career college is in the process of launching a new business course. The course coordinator learns that a renowned lecturer and expert in the field has unexpectedly become available and has expressed interest in teaching the course.

Having this individual involved with the course is likely to lead to an increase in enrollments, demand, and profitability.

To exploit this opportunity, the budget for the course will have to be increased. The objectives with regard to the course structure and layout may also have to be revised and altered.

Exploiting an opportunity can be expensive in terms of costs, time, and other resources. So it's important to assess the benefits of exploiting an opportunity in relation to the expense of obtaining it.

It's generally accepted that you should try to exploit opportunities before you attempt to share, enhance, or accept them.

Exploiting an opportunity involves trying to earn as much benefit from it as possible. Sometimes, though, it can make more sense to share an opportunity. This involves joining with an external party to increase the chance of securing benefits, and agreeing to share the rewards.

For example, suppose a manufacturing company wants to extend its sales into an overseas market. To minimize the risk, the business development manager negotiates a partnership with an international marketing and distribution company. This company already has experience and an existing infrastructure in the overseas market.

Sharing the risk of entering the new market with this company improves the manufacturer's chance of success. The possible reward of going it alone would likely be larger but the risk of failure is much lower this way.

**Question**

Which statements are examples of exploiting and sharing an opportunity?

**Options:**

1. You increase the number of employees in the order fulfillment division when an advertising campaign is launched
2. You partner with a specialist company when developing a new product
3. You request a written warranty when purchasing expensive electronic equipment
4. You use a reputable supplier to supply you with crucial materials

**Answer**

Option 1: This option is correct. This is an example of exploiting an opportunity. There may be extra orders after an advertising campaign. You need to be able to fulfill those orders to exploit the opportunity.

Option 2: This option is correct. This is an example of sharing an opportunity. You increase your chance of success by developing a new product with a specialist company.

Option 3: This option is incorrect. This is an example of transferring a threat, not exploiting or sharing an opportunity.

Option 4: This option is incorrect. This is an example of mitigating a threat, not exploiting or sharing an opportunity.

## *Enhancing and accepting opportunities*

Another way of responding to an opportunity is to enhance it. Whereas exploiting an opportunity means making sure it definitely happens, enhancing means increasing its probability and positive impact.

For example, the owner of a factory could take active steps to win the approval of nearby residents by donating funds for local projects. This may enhance support for the factory and, in turn, increase the profits derived from local residents – who may become regular purchasers of its products.

Similarly, a manager who plans to restructure a department might devote considerable time to meeting all affected employees and discussing the situation with them one-to-one. This may enhance employee support for the new initiative – which increases the likelihood of it being implemented successfully.

Another option when responding to an opportunity is to accept it. For this response, you take no specific action to address the opportunity. Instead, you hope you'll get lucky and that the opportunity will occur without any outside intervention.

Consider this situation. A small plumbing supply company has started supplying a major player in the building industry. The sales manager at the plumbing company realizes that the company could secure further deals through the building contractor. However, being too pushy for additional business could annoy or scare off the client. So the sales manager decides it's best to continue providing good service and just to accept any extra contracts should they be offered.

**Question**

Which statements are examples of enhancing or accepting an opportunity?

**Options:**

1. You organize a team meeting to reassure employees and increase support for an upcoming merger

2. You don't promote a new service but hope people will hear about it by word of mouth

3. You decide not to do business with a subcontractor who has a history of delivering work late

4. You request a guarantee when purchasing an expensive new product

**Answer**

Option 1: This option is correct. Organizing a team meeting to reassure employees and increase support for a merger is an example of enhancing an opportunity. Enhancement involves taking steps to increase the likelihood of an opportunity occurring – or if it does occur, to increase the positive impact of the opportunity on your organization.

Option 2: This option is correct. Not promoting a new service but instead relying on word of mouth is an example of accepting an opportunity. Acceptance involves taking no specific action. Instead, you hope you'll get lucky and that the opportunity will occur without any outside intervention.

Option 3: This option is incorrect. Not doing business with a subcontractor who has an unreliable work history is an example of avoiding a threat, not enhancing or accepting an opportunity.

Option 4: This option is incorrect. Requesting a guarantee for an expensive new product is an example of transferring a threat, not enhancing or accepting an opportunity.

**Question**

Match each method of responding to an opportunity to its corresponding example.

**Options:**
A. Share
B. Exploit
C. Enhance
D. Accept

**Targets:**
1. Establish a new business venture with an experienced partner

2. Hire additional workers to speed up production so you can deliver shipments in time for a busy sales period

3. Improve the chances of hiring skilled workers by running shuttle buses to remote towns

4. Ignore subsidiary cost savings because they may help cover cost overruns later in the project

**Answer**

Establishing a new business venture with an experienced partner is an example of sharing an opportunity. This approach involves joining with another party to increase the chance of benefiting from an opportunity. Both parties then share the risks and the potential rewards.

Hiring additional workers to speed up production so you can deliver shipments in time for a busy sales period is an example of exploiting an opportunity. Exploiting an opportunity ensures that it occurs.

By running shuttle buses to remote towns, you enhance the opportunity of hiring more qualified staff. This increases the likelihood of benefits from the opportunity.

Ignoring subsidiary cost savings because they may help cover cost overruns later is an example of accepting an opportunity. While you acknowledge the opportunity, you don't prepare a particular response to share, exploit, or enhance it.

## When to use each response

When dealing with risk, you may be tempted to focus exclusively on the threats your organization is facing. This is usually a mistake, as it could cause you to overlook many exciting opportunities. You already know there are various ways of responding to opportunities, such as by exploiting, sharing, enhancing, or accepting them. It's important to understand when exactly you should use each of these different response types.

When you encounter an opportunity, it's usually a good idea to decide whether it can be exploited before you consider any other response. This is the most assertive way of responding to an opportunity, as it makes the opportunity you're dealing with inevitable. It aims to increase the probability of the opportunity occurring to as close to 100% as possible.

If an opportunity has a high probability of occurring and carries with it a range of potential benefits, you should generally choose to exploit it. This kind of opportunity may offer high-impact benefits that your organization simply can't afford to miss it, such as the opportunity to increase revenues or grow sales.

If you can't exploit an opportunity, you should try to enhance it yourself. This involves taking specific steps to increase the probability that the opportunity will actually occur, as well as increasing its potential impact.

To enhance an opportunity, identify the conditions that trigger it. Then work to reinforce and strengthen those conditions.

For example, an opportunity to win an award for outstanding service could be triggered by the number of customer votes you receive in an online survey. You could strengthen this trigger by e-mailing all your customers and stating how much you'd appreciate their votes.

If you can't exploit an opportunity or enhance it yourself, consider sharing it with another party. Sharing involves allocating ownership of the opportunity to a third party who is able to handle it best – and extract the maximum benefit from it.

Try to share opportunities with people who already have a vested interest in the project's success, such as the client or sponsor. This makes it more likely that they'll take responsibility for the various opportunities identified. Risk-sharing partnerships, special-purpose companies, or joint ventures can all be established to share opportunities.

As a manager, sharing opportunities doesn't mean that you abdicate responsibility for a project's success. Instead, you should stay actively involved in ensuring that the opportunities being shared are actually realized.

The final response you should consider when dealing with an opportunity is to accept it. If an opportunity can't be exploited, shared, or enhanced, you may have no choice but to accept it. If the opportunity is minor, doesn't offer any significant benefits, or is too expensive to address, you might choose to respond in this way.

Just like when accepting a threat, you can accept an opportunity in a passive or active way. Passive acceptance involves ignoring the opportunity, but hoping it will occur.

Active acceptance involves taking no special action to make the opportunity happen. However, you develop a contingency plan that sets out what you will do if the opportunity does occur.

**Question**

Match each response type to the opportunity it addresses most effectively.

**Options:**
A. Exploit
B. Share
C. Enhance
D. Accept

**Targets:**
1. An opportunity that's likely to happen and offers significant revenue benefits to your organization
2. An opportunity you can't enhance by yourself that could benefit project stakeholders

3. An opportunity where you can take steps to improve the probability of it occurring yourself but you can't share it

4. A minor opportunity that's too expensive to address and doesn't offer any real benefits

**Answer**

An opportunity that's likely to happen and offers significant revenue benefits should be exploited. Exploitation aims to increase the probability of the opportunity occurring to as close to 100% as possible.

An opportunity you can't enhance yourself that could benefit project stakeholders should be shared. It's a good idea to share opportunities with people who already have a vested interest in the project's success.

If you can't exploit an opportunity but can take steps to improve the probability of it occurring yourself, you should aim to enhance the opportunity. To do this, identify the conditions that cause the opportunity. Then work to reinforce and strengthen those conditions.

A minor opportunity that's too expensive to address and doesn't offer any real benefits should be accepted. You can accept an opportunity in a passive or active way.

## Considering possible responses

When dealing with an opportunity, always examine the various responses you could make before deciding on the best course of action. Consider Maggie's situation. She's the marketing manager at an insurance company. A competitor has just ceased trading, leaving a huge gap in the life insurance market. As a result, Maggie is certain an opportunity now exists to sells thousands of new life insurance policies. She estimates this could increase her company's revenues by $1 million this year alone.

Maggie considers her choices. She could exploit the opportunity by launching a targeted advertising campaign to promote her organization's life insurance policies to new customers. This option would be expensive – it could cost upward of $200,000. And it means her existing marketing plans for the year would have to change. But Maggie is confident her organization will gain significant benefits in terms of increased sales and revenues.

Alternatively, Maggie could share the opportunity by partnering with a company that specializes in life insurance. This option means another company would share in the expense of the advertising campaign. However, the other company would also share in the potential benefits.

Maggie has other choices. For example, she could try to enhance the opportunity by writing to all her existing customers and stating they'll receive a discount if they recommend her organization to new life insurance customers.

Finally, Maggie could accept the opportunity, but decide to take no action at all. She might simply hope that new clients contact her organization when it comes to replacing or purchasing new life insurance policies.

Maggie considers all her options. Because the opportunity she's facing is likely to have a significant impact on her organization in terms of increased revenues, she knows she can justify the expense of launching an expensive advertising campaign. The opportunity is also certain to occur. So Maggie decides the best response is to exploit the opportunity she's dealing with.

**Question**

Imagine you're the sales manager in a company that produces small electronic devices. You've identified a possible business opportunity – you think there may be untapped sources of revenue within your existing customer base. According to your research, there's a reasonable chance you could upsell to about a fifth of your existing customers. This could increase revenues by $200,000 annually. However, you're not sure if your calculations are correct.

How should you respond to this opportunity?

**Options:**

1. Invest $3 million in a range of add-on products that should appeal to existing customers

2. Form a five-year partnership, at a cost of $300,000 a year, with a marketing company to promote your products more forcefully to customers

3. Advise your customer support employees about upselling techniques they could use

4. Hope customers are impressed with your products and choose to buy more

**Answer**

Option 1: This option is incorrect. The opportunity you're dealing with is uncertain. And you aren't sure if your calculations are correct. In such situations, exploiting the opportunity by investing a large sum of money isn't an appropriate response.

Option 2: This option is incorrect. Sharing the opportunity by forming a partnership with an expensive third party isn't recommended in this situation. Any possible revenue increases could be offset by the cost of the partnership.

Option 3: This is the correct option. For this opportunity, your best approach is to try to enhance it yourself. This involves increasing the probability that the opportunity will actually occur, as well as increasing its potential impact.

Option 4: This option is incorrect. The opportunity you're dealing with can be enhanced in a cost- effective way. So you shouldn't simply accept it and hope for the best.

## Contingency Planning

Contingent response strategies involve planning responses in case risk events actually occur. They also involve assigning reserves so that the responses can be implemented when necessary.

To determine the size of the reserves you should set aside, calculate the expected monetary value – or EMV – of each risk. To calculate the EMV for a risk, multiply its probability by its estimated impact, in terms of cost or time. Then add the EMVs for all the risks identified and express the result as a positive value. This gives you the required contingency reserve.

After you've responded to the risks of a project, it's important to evaluate each stage in the risk management, or RM, process.

## Benefits of contingency planning

In times of crisis, "could have" and "would have" aren't words that customers or senior management appreciate. Imagine reporting to your manager that output from a production facility has halved – all because you didn't set aside enough time or money to train employees to use new equipment during planning. Looking back, you can see that a backup plan could have helped, and extra cash might have helped prevent the crisis.

The use of contingent response strategies is an important option to consider when deciding how to respond to risk. This approach is an active form of risk acceptance.

Also known as contingency planning, contingent response strategies involve planning responses in case risk events actually occur. They also involve assigning reserves so that the responses can be implemented when necessary.

Reserves are usually sums of money, but can include time, materials, and staff. They're any resources needed to offset the impact a risk event has on a project's scope, schedule, cost, or quality.

Sometimes it's not possible or cost effective to respond to a risk until the risk actually occurs. This is where contingency planning comes in. Consider Taku's situation. He's heard a rumor that a competitor is developing a new software product that would directly compete with his own organization's flagship product. This could negatively impact sales in Taku's organization. However, the new product may never materialize. Taku accepts the risk. But he also develops a contingency plan.

Six months later, Taku gets an unwelcome surprise. The competitor's product appears on the market. And it directly competes with his own company's product. However, because Taku has a contingency plan, he knows exactly how to respond.

Taku has identified several additional features that can be quickly incorporated into his company's product. His team starts work right away, and a new version is ready for release within a couple of weeks. The new features help it outsell the competitor's product.

As a result of Taku's ability to think ahead and be decisive, his organization experiences minimal disruption. And sales continue to increase.

## *Examples of contingency planning*

Contingency planning doesn't involve mitigating risks by reducing the likelihood that they'll occur. But it also doesn't mean just ignoring the risks. Instead it involves ensuring plans and resources are in place if the risks occur. Where appropriate, it can be used to deal with a threat or an opportunity.

**Threat**

Operations within a manufacturing company are at risk of a proposed change in environmental legislation. If a new law is passed, it will require the company to invest heavily in more energy- efficient equipment, or face penalties.

So the operations manager develops an equipment purchase plan and assigns a cash reserve to implement the plan, in case the law is passed.

**Opportunity**

A proposed law requiring the purchase of new energy-efficient equipment poses an opportunity as well as a threat to a manufacturing company. If passed, the law will enable the company to qualify for tax incentives. The better the company complies with environmental requirements, the bigger the tax incentives will be.

So the operations manager considers the benefit of assigning a large monetary reserve to ensure that the company can comply at the top level and receive the highest tax incentives, if the law is passed.

The level of risk for which you create contingency plans should depend largely on stakeholders' risk tolerance. Suppose you'll lose a key contract if a certain risk event occurs. This means your risk tolerance is low. You would create solid contingency plans for this risk event. But in a project with a very flexible schedule, you might think twice before applying contingency planning to a risk that would delay the project only by a few days.

It's important to monitor a project for impending risk events so you can implement contingency plans in time. To assist with monitoring, you can identify warning signs – or triggers – to watch out for.

A trigger might be a threshold value of a performance metric such as cost performance or a threshold defect rate. For example, if your costs increase by 10% in one year, or more than 1% of your products are found to be defective, you may have exceeded threshold values in these areas. Other triggers could be missing a milestone or a change in a business relationship.

Whatever the trigger, it should be clearly defined in the contingency plan and tracked during the project.

**Question**

A chosen supplier for a project offers the lowest costs. However, there's a risk that this supplier could shut down during the course of the project.

Which response to the risk illustrates the appropriate use of a contingent response strategy?

**Options:**

1. You create a plan, with budgetary and time reserves, for buying materials from the next preferred supplier on your list, although this supplier is more expensive

2. You accept the risk and plan to respond to it as it affects the project

3. You try to transfer the risk to the supplier, who is facing bankruptcy, by insisting that this supplier honors the supply contract

4. At the start of the project, you submit a request to change the product scope by switching to a material that is available from a number of lower-quality suppliers

**Answer**

Option 1: This is the correct option. By developing a plan and allocating reserves, you ensure you can respond appropriately if the risk of losing a key supplier actually occurs.

Option 2: This option is incorrect. Passively accepting the risk, without defining a clear plan or allocating reserves to cover it, isn't an example of a contingent response strategy.

Option 3: This option is incorrect. This response doesn't indicate that you've developed a sensible contingency plan, or set aside any reserves to handle the risk.

Option 4: This option is incorrect. This response involves an attempt to mitigate the risk by eliminating the risk cause. A contingent response strategy would involve planning and assigning reserves for handling the risk only if and when it does occur.

## Calculating the contingency reserve

An important part of contingency planning is setting aside enough reserves to put the planned responses in motion when risk events occur. But how big should the reserves be that you set aside? A statistical method for determining this is expected monetary value – or EMV – analysis.

To calculate the EMV for a risk, you multiply its probability by its estimated impact, in terms of cost or time. You estimate the probability and impact of risks during the second stage of risk management – assessing risk.

So, for instance, if a positive risk event, or opportunity, has a 5% probability of occurring and would result in a gain of $20,000, its EMV would be $1,000. This would be recorded as a positive EMV.

A risk's impact is a negative value if it will cost a project time or money. So if a risk, or threat, is 9% likely to cost your project $15,000, you multiply 0.09 by -$15,000, and obtain an EMV of -$1,350.

The net EMV is the sum of the EMVs for all the risks you've identified.

The net EMV will be negative if the threats outweigh the opportunities, or positive if opportunities outweigh the threats.

If the threats outweigh the opportunities, and the net EMV is negative – which is -$350 in this example – you convert this into the positive total value required as a contingency reserve. So the contingency reserve in this case is $350.

### Question
Which formula should you use to calculate the EMV for a risk?
**Options:**
1. EMV = Probability × Impact
2. EMV = Probability – Impact
3. EMV = Probability + Impact

### Answer
To calculate the EMV for a risk, you need to multiply its

probability by its estimated impact, in terms of cost or time.

Consider a phase in a building project. The threat of losing both senior engineers has a probability of 10% and could cost the project $110,000. So its EMV is -$11,000. Similarly, you determine that the threat of disruptions due to severe weather conditions is about 25% and may cost $275,000. This risk has an EMV of -$68,750.

There's a 50% probability of a new health and safety law being passed. This could cost the project $105,000 in fines. So this threat has an EMV of -$52,500.

If the new law is passed, the project stands to qualify for government subsidies worth $200,000. The probability that the law will be passed is still 50%, giving you a positive EMV of $100,000.

You've calculated the individual EMVs for each threat and opportunity. By adding the EMVs you obtain a net EMV for the phase. The net EMV is -$32,250. So you set aside a contingency reserve of $32,250 to cover the costs of meeting the threats and exploiting the opportunity that you've identified.

### Question
Then match the correct EMV value to each risk. Not all EMV values will have a match.

**Options:**
A. -$10,000
B. -$1,500 C. $500
D. -$500 E. $10,000

**Targets:**
1. Threat of not reaching Milestone A on schedule
2. Threat of an interest rate hike
3. Opportunity for predicted cut in fuel prices

Answer

The threat of not reaching Milestone A has an EMV of -$10,000. You get this value by multiplying 10% by -$100,000.

The threat of an interest rate hike has an EMV of -$1,500. You get this value by multiplying 15% by -$10,000.

The opportunity for a predicted cut in fuel prices has an EMV of $500. To calculate this value, you multiply 5% by $10,000.

**Question**

Based on the information in the table, what is the required contingency reserve for the project?

A table illustrates that the threat of not reaching Milestone A on schedule has a 10% probability, an impact of -$100,000, and an EMV of -$10,000. An interest rate hike is 15% likely, has an impact of -$10,000, and an EMV of -$1,500. The opportunity for a cut in fuel prices has a 5% probability, an impact of $10,000, and an EMV of $500.

Options:
1. $11,000
2. -$11,000
3. $100,000
4. $12,000

**Answer**

Option 1: This is the correct option. When you add each EMV value, the net EMV is -$11,000. The contingency reserve is the positive expression of the net EMV, which is $11,000.

Option 2: This option is incorrect. The value of the net EMV for the project is -$11,000, not the required contingency reserve. The contingency reserve is always expressed as a positive value, and in this case it's $11,000.

Option 3: This option is incorrect. You've added the impact costs and expressed the result as a positive value. You should have added the EMV for each risk. This gives you a net EMV of -$11,000, so the contingency reserve is $11,000.

Option 4: This option is incorrect. The third risk in the table has a positive EMV, not a negative one. Adding the three EMV values gives you a net EMV of -$11,000. So the contingency reserve is $11,000.

Some threats and opportunities require time-based contingency plans. For instance, the impacts of network failures are usually measured in terms of the downtime they cause, rather

RISK MANAGEMENT

than in direct financial costs.

If you include a contingency reserve in the schedule for a project, it helps ensure delays associated with risk events can be absorbed.

To calculate the required schedule contingency reserve for a project, you use the EMV analysis method but use time values rather than monetary values.

Suppose you're managing an IT project to develop a database. You predict a 30% risk that you'll discover the project is more complex than you planned, and this will add 40 days to the schedule. The EMV for this threat is 30% of -40, which is -12 days.

Similarly, the threat of downtime from IT failure gives you an EMV of -2 days. So with a net EMV of -14 days, you add a contingency reserve of 14 days to the schedule.

**Question**

You are the accounting manager in a small company that provides legal services. You want to introduce a new financial reporting system in your department. You've identified the risks and opportunities involved, their probabilities, and their impacts.

What contingency reserve should you set aside for the project?

A table showing that the threat of under-estimating the level of expertise needed to master the new system has a probability of 40% and an impact of -50 days. The threat of losing data during the transfer to the new system has a probability of 30% and an impact of -20 days. The opportunity to generate financial reports more quickly has a probability of 60% and an impact of 30 days.

**Options:**
1. 8 days
2. -8 days
3. 44 days
4. 4 days

**Answer**

Option 1: This is the correct option. After calculations, 40% of -50 is -20; 30% of -20 is -6; 60% of 30 is 18. When you add these three EMVs, you get a net EMV of -8. So the contingency reserve is

8 days.

Option 2: This option is incorrect. When you add the EMV for each threat and opportunity, you get a net EMV of -8. However, the contingency reserve is always expressed as a positive value, so in this case it's 8 days.

Option 3: This option is incorrect. The opportunity to generate reports more quickly has a positive EMV of 18 days, not a negative one. When you add the EMV for each risk, you add -20, -6, and 18, which gives -8. So the contingency reserve is 8 days.

Option 4: This option is incorrect. The threat of losing data during the transfer to the new system has a negative EMV of -6, not a positive one. So when you add the EMV for each risk, you add -20, -6, and 18, which gives -8. So the contingency reserve is 8 days.

## Monitoring the RM process

After you've decided how to respond to the risks of a project, it's important to monitor the overall risk management – or RM – process in an effective way. You can do this by evaluating the effectiveness of each stage in the process. You may recall that the first stage is to identify the risks you're dealing with. Stage two is to assess the risks you've identified. And at stage three you deal with the risks.

You can ask yourself some questions to find out how well you've handled each stage. To evaluate the first stage, ask yourself, "Were all the risks identified?" To evaluate stage two, ask the question, "Was the risk assessment effective?" And to evaluate the third stage, ask, "Were the responses effective?"

If your answers to any of these questions are negative, be sure to analyze the reasons and document any lessons you've learned. This knowledge may benefit other colleagues who deal with risk in your organization. And it should help you manage risk more effectively in the future.

www.ingramcontent.com/pod-product-compliance
Lightning Source LLC
Chambersburg PA
CBHW031928240526
45464CB00023B/2168